Embrace

The Child Within

by

Rose La Rose

DORRANCE
PUBLISHING CO
EST. 1920
PITTSBURGH, PENNSYLVANIA 15238

The contents of this work, including, but not limited to, the accuracy of events, people, and places depicted; opinions expressed; permission to use previously published materials included; and any advice given or actions advocated are solely the responsibility of the author, who assumes all liability for said work and indemnifies the publisher against any claims stemming from publication of the work.

Dorrance Publishing Co
585 Alpha Drive
Suite 103
Pittsburgh, PA 15238
Visit our website at *www.dorrancebookstore.com*

ISBN: 978-1-6491-3109-6
eISBN: 978-1-6491-3616-9

I would like to dedicate this memoir to my psychologist/doctor that encouraged me to write. The hometown officer who validated and gave the 4-year-old child a voice. She helped me get through the traumatic experience. She is the patron officer of children. Also, first and foremost, my husband Barry for his continued non-judgemental support I needed to accomplish this mission. Our daughter, Melissa, for triggering the repressed memory, and the rest is history. The love that I took from this experience is to embrace the child within.

About This Book

The stories in this book reflect the author's recollection of events. The names, locations, and identifying characteristics have been changed to protect the privacy of those depicted. Dialogue has been re-created from memory.

Part 1

That Night

Chapter 1

I was four years old when I went up to bed with Darla for the night. Our bedroom was set up to fit bunk beds, a twin, and a full-size bed. It was just a simple room with an old linoleum floor. On one of the walls hung an art project my older brother, James, had made at a church bazaar. James was about 13 years old at that time. The child's art was on purple construction paper with words in silver glitter. I liked this wall hanging. I was able to read the words. This was a child's prayer. We kids were playing, laughing, and jumping on beds upstairs when I asked James if I could have the wall hanging.

James said, *"You can have the wall hanging, just leave it where it is."*

I said, *"I want to take this to our new house when we move for our new room."*

My sister Darla interjected, *"You shouldn't have that. Only a person that can read should have that. You can't read"*

I stood on the bed and placed my hand on the art hanging. In my little voice I read the words out loud. Everyone became quiet.

Now I lay me down to sleep.
I pray the Lord my soul to keep.
If I should die before I wake,
I pray the Lord my soul to take.
Amen!

· · · · ·

After I read that, the other kids were saying, in quiet astonishment, *"Graci can read!"* Darla and I were left in the room alone and we went to bed for the night. Our twin bed was pushed up against the wall elongated. I climbed in bed first—closest to the wall—and Darla got in after me to lie down. We lay head to head as always. As I turned to the left, I saw Pa standing at the bedside. We referred to our father as "Pa" or "Poppy," while the older kids referred to him as "the old man." When I looked up at Pa, he started talking and singing songs in Spanish. He kept constant eye contact with me.

As soon as he finished his song, I said, *"Sing one more."*

He told me he couldn't. *"Darla is crying."*

Because I couldn't hear her cry, I didn't think she was, *"No, she's not crying! Stay and sing one more."*

I thought he was trying to trick me and not sing anymore. He did sing another song though. After three songs he stopped singing and looked down to his right at Darla. He broke his eye contact with me.

While looking down to his right at Darla, he again said slyly, with an evil giggle, *"Darla is crying."*

I turned my head to the left to look at her and she had her right arm over her eyes. I asked doubtfully, *"Darla are you crying?"*

Darla lifted the crook of her elbow and opened her eyes real big like they were popping out of her head. She looked right at me. Her eyes were full of anger, all red and watery. I asked her again, *"Darla why are you crying?"*

Darla didn't answer and put her arm back down. When I did the same, Pa moved away from the bed, turned around, and headed out of the room downstairs. I saw Darla crying. I said out loud she was crying. Why didn't he help her? I was confused. He didn't help her.

I was lying in the bed on my side and kept looking toward the door. I heard a lot of noise like someone was flying up the stairs. I saw my two older sisters, Marie and Rosey, coming into the bedroom. Marie was in her late 20s at that time and Rosey was about 14. They hurriedly walked over to the foot of the bed and stood there behind the footboard. I kept looking at the stairs. I saw my mother coming up and behind her was another sister, Dora.

My mother walked over to the bedside where Pa had been standing. She stood farther away from the bed than where Pa was. Dora was lingering around

4

the top of the stairs to my left. I heard my mother say, *"We were coming home and saw Pa coming down from upstairs. What was he doing up here?"*

Darla threw back the covers and jumped out of bed. I stood up on the bed with my back against the wall. Darla stood next to mother's left side. My mother reached her left hand out for Darla to hold with her right hand. Now they were both facing me.

Darla began crying while screaming at me and stomping her foot. *"Graci kept telling him to stay and sing."*

I began to cry. *"I didn't know! I didn't know!"*

Dora was coming at me from the left with an open raised hand. Her short, black, wiry hair was parted on the side. She looked scary. Her face was red with a wrinkled nose and clenched teeth. She looked like a sea creature coming out of Lake Erie. She was ready to lean over and start slapping me when my mother said, *"Dora—don't hit her! She didn't know!"*

Dora wanted to continue, but Mother stopped her. *"You hear what Darla is saying?"* *"No, she didn't know."* Dora was validating Darla.

I didn't even know what it was that I didn't know. I felt I had to say something.

Rosey and Marie were quietly standing to my right. They didn't say a word to help me. My mother and Darla were standing in front of me holding hands. Darla was hysterically crying. She was wearing a knee-length white cotton nightgown, screaming and crying at me, *"Gracie kept telling him to stay and sing!"* Her long dark brown wavy hair looked sweaty. It was falling down her pale, ashy-white skin. Darla's legs looked long and lanky with big knees as she stomped her foot screaming at me.

Surrounded and cornered by all these people, my back was literally up against the wall. I had nowhere else to go. No one there was doing anything to help me. I felt my mother's voice wasn't going to be strong enough to hold Dora back. I left myself standing there. I learned later that this was a defense mechanism I involuntarily used to dissociate from trauma. Someone there that night had to know something went horribly wrong. I left myself just standing there. I saw myself, as an observer, draw a blank stare. I suddenly became quiet. This is how I dissociated from what was happening around me.

Before that night, I was a lively little chatterbox. I loved talking to people and excited most of the time. After I left, I became silent. I don't remember anything else that happened after that point. I couldn't say if the light was on or off anymore. It was on during all of the commotion and noise. I was just gone, vanished.

. . . . .

Dissociation, in general, does not last for a very long time, particularly when children experience it. Unfortunately, my case was different from others. My dissociation lasted for years. It didn't have to. All someone in my family had to do was talk to me. They wouldn't. They wanted to act like that night never occurred and never spoke of that evil again. Not to me anyway. They acted all la-de-da. As they got older, the more arrogant they became. I think they actually believed they were better than me. They treated me like I didn't exist. They never wanted to tell me anything. Especially Darla and Dora. Darla was always afraid I'd acknowledge something bad had happened. Dora was just out to get me in any way she knew how. She is the one that always said, *"Graci is spoiled and nobody wants her around."* Yet, years later when her husband died and the insurance funds were gone, she wanted to come and live with me. Not a chance. She created too many problems for herself. The two of us could never be happy under the same roof. Not even in the same state.

Dissociation causes memory gaps. It did not impact my memory any differently. I had localized amnesia dissociation. That memory left me and went into an inaccessible part of my memory. With localized amnesia, a specific traumatic event is erased from memory and cannot be remembered. I left myself and that included my identity, thought process, insight, and my perception was not keen as it is now. I was left a lost soul at age four and had to go through a huge portion of my life this way. Had I been taken out of that toxic environment where there was little to no stress, I would probably have remembered that trauma a lot sooner than I did. I'd have saved myself a lot of heartache and grief. There are big gaps in my memory over parts of my life. One of my older sisters told me that they always thought I wasn't paying attention. I got the impression that she thought they were reading me wrong. I was this lively little inquisitive precocious chatterbox up until that traumatic moment in the bedroom. Still, I carried on in life.

Chapter 2

I was thirteenth out of the fourteen children our parents had. When I was a child, I grew up with eight siblings in the house. By the time I was born, the other six were grownups and had moved out. There was a generation gap among the children that mirrored the kind of generational gap you have with your parents. There was the '50s rock-n-roll period, '60s counterculture, and the hippie period of the '70s which is where I fall. I was the youngest sister, so I was the baby of the girls, and the only brother younger than me was the baby of the boys. That's how Ma introduced us to her friends.

The older kids gave us the younger ones a hard time. Maybe because the economics of the family were tougher on them than for us. Since the six older ones had moved out and married, our parent's budget had loosened a great deal while I was growing up. Some of my siblings even moved to other states and barely visited us. That would be the older six that lived in Mexico. My older brothers all had successful careers as machinists or worked in the ship-yards, steel industry, or automobile factories.

All of the sisters in my family are five years apart with me being the young-est. Starting with the night I dissociated and from the oldest to the youngest in hierarchical order, there is Marie (28), Yvonne (24), Dora (19), Rosey (14), Darla (9), and me (4). Dora was recently married back then and was soon to move out. I really don't remember her living with us. She was one of the older six that was born in Mexico. All of the boys are five years apart too. My mother had a child every two years and described us as "stair-steps." It went boy, girl,

7

boy, girl, boy, etc. Darla and Dora had a very weird relationship. The only time they would be friends is when they teamed up against me. My brother Vaughn, who was seven years older than me, would join them, too.

With long black hair, deep sweet eyes, and a dark complexion, I was a pretty child. Someone who had sharp, yet small, features. Also, my mother always paid a lot of attention to how we looked so we would always be well-dressed. My mother was of Italian heritage and my father was Mexican. My parents met in Indiana where they married. They married in the '30s, the era of the Great Depression. My father and mother moved to Mexico after getting married. They already had a child who they took to Mexico with them. By the time they came back to the U.S., and thirteen years later, my parents had six children altogether. The six older children spoke only Spanish when they returned to the states. They were placed back a grade or two in school to learn English. That was not uncommon in those days. In fact, if a child was of school age and came from a different country and spoke a different language, hence, not English, being placed back a grade or more was to be expected, in order for that child to learn English. That's how they dealt with that back then.

I always admired my mother. She was smart and was great with languages. She spoke Italian, Spanish, and English and I enthusiastically would say, *my mother is trilingual*. She was a lively person and loved to play music. She looked so amazing playing the piano. She was short and plump in the stomach with short wavy salt and pepper hair. She told me that she was thin when she was younger and gained weight after she had her sixth child. Anyone can tell she was petite at one time. Everyone in her family is. She used to pull her hair back in a loose bun and was very soft spoken. Her voice barely rose above a whisper. She was intelligent and responsible. My father was a lucky man. My mother even took care of everyone medically when they lived in Mexico. When she lived there with the older children, she had to be everyone's doctor as the family couldn't afford to visit one. She had to be quite resourceful with everything.

Living in a different country with a different language and culture couldn't have been easy. Mother learned Spanish after she got to Mexico and became fluent. She took great care of everybody. When I was growing up, I remember she sewed aprons to sell and cleaned homes and other places to supplement the household income. She even tried to sell Avon.

Pa was born in Mexico and raised in an orphanage there. He spoke both Spanish and English. He was smart in that way. I remember him as an older man with salt and pepper colored very short to-the-scalp hair. He had a light complexion. He was of short stature and round around the stomach. He kind of reminded me of a bowling pin. I never met anyone in his family. They all lived in Mexico. When I was growing up, he and my mother spoke Spanish to each other, but used English to communicate with the children. The older children who were born in Mexico had to focus on learning English and eventually became bilingual too. I admire just about anyone that can speak more than one language.

My father worked for U.S. Steel as a laborer when I was growing up. He also worked as a carpenter on the side. He was an alcoholic, and I later learned, a tyrannical father. My oldest sister Marie told me, when they lived in Mexico, he'd put chains around the ankles and wrists of the children and whip them with a strap. Living in Mexico back in the day, no one cared. My mother was lost and didn't have any help. Eventually, her mother, my grandmother, had a younger daughter, my aunt, go to Mexico to get my mother and bring her back to the states. After 13 years of living in Mexico, my mother, father and the older six kids did return to the states. By then, my mother was traumatized too. Pa had tuberculosis and doctors had put him into remission. He was in and out of the sanitarium throughout his life. I remember us kids visiting him at the sanitarium. We couldn't go inside to visit. We'd stay outside and play while he'd come to a window and stand there with my mother. He'd look out at us so we could see him.

Some weekends Pa would dress nicely in his best clothes and wear a fancy long black cashmere coat. I never knew where he went. He was just gone for a long time. I don't remember seeing him return home either. Sometimes on weekends, he'd go to a baseball game alone. My mother bought him gifts on his birthday. I remember her giving him a transistor radio one year. Another year she gave him a radio for their bedroom. He listened to the baseball games on his radio. On New Year's Eve, he would get all dressed up with his long black coat and go out to a bar. He would celebrate the New Year there. Once he brought home a bag of used New Year's Eve noisemakers. He never took my mother with him. He would just disappear for a long time. He was a mysterious man.

Chapter 3

I don't like being bound to any nationality, religion, or gender in the traditional sense. Since I was raised American, I did not have to follow any specific culture, unlike my older siblings. Fortunately, my parents never forced me to choose. I don't see why anyone has to be bound to any culture, religion, sex, or gender. That should be a personal preference and best left to that person. There is nothing wrong either way. I know that I used to catch a lot of flak for not speaking Spanish. Mostly from the Hispanic/Latino community.

My parents were in their forties at the time of my birth. With the girls from oldest to youngest was Marie, Yvonne, Dora, Rosey, Darla, and me. Marie, Yvonne, Dora, and Darla were all short with black hair and brown eyes. Darla actually had brown hair. Marie, Dora, and Darla had a lighter complexion when compared to the rest of us. They were probably three shades lighter than me. Yvonne, Rosey and I were of dark complexion. I am the tallest girl at 5'4, and the others were barely over 5 feet. I was a tall giant compared to them. We are all petite.

When I was ten years old, Yvonne died in an auto related accident. She had been missing for two weeks. My mother was looking all over for her and calling around. My mother received a call one day to go to a hospital to identify a young girl that was found dead from carbon monoxide poisoning and was brought into the hospital. A lady that worked there called my mother. She knew my mother was looking for Yvonne. That had to have broken her heart. I can't even imagine. Mother told me, when she got back home, they pulled the sheet off of the young girl. She immediately saw Yvonne's long black hair falling down. This happened in Indiana's below zero, ice cold January's winter in the early 1960s. My mother told me a detective told her that he found her frozen body in a car parked in a garage that belonged to the young man. She was in the front seat of the car with her head resting on the steering wheel and arms clenched around the wheel. The young man was frozen in the back seat of the auto. My mother did her own investigative work to find out what happened. She learned that Yvonne was at a New Year's Eve party and was the only one sober to drive. She drove this young man's car, as he was passed out in the back seat, and dropped off her other friends at their homes, then took this young man home. He was missing at work for two weeks when someone finally checked his house and saw his car in the garage. She was only 26 and left behind two children. Carolyn, five, and Martin, nine months. My mother took them in and became their legal guardian. Yvonne had never married their father.

Shortly after that bitter January, my mother received a notice in the mail for Yvonne. The letter was letting her know that she passed the nursing exam to enter a nursing program in our hometown. My mother was devastated and her heart broke once again. Marie was lost more than before and became even more quiet. Yvonne and Marie did everything they could together. Marie told me that Yvonne was her best friend. My mother must have had a heart made of tiny broken pieces glued together. I was just quiet and numb not thinking I wouldn't be seeing Yvonne anymore. Dissociation held my emotions captive.

· · · · ·

Before the night of the traumatic incident that was inflicted on me, I was considered a happy child. I was somebody who loved to talk and was known to be excited most of the time. My oldest sister Marie would usually come along with her husband, Heller. Marie was a housewife and worked in some of the factories throughout her life. She went to cosmetology school and worked as a hairdresser from her home. She wore her hair in a black beehive. She would sit in the kitchen when she'd come over or would help Ma. Our kitchen was huge and our parent's bedroom was off to the side of it. As I remember the kitchen was probably the biggest room of the house after my parent's bedroom.

The kitchen had a decent-sized counter table with eight chairs, four on each side. That was where the adults gathered. Whenever Marie came to visit, Heller, would be with her. Heller was an average height man and worked at the steel plant. When he visited, he would look for me and have me seated on his lap. He would constantly talk to me and teach me new things. I was told that I had started to speak fluently when I was three years old. Unlike most children of that age, I could communicate in full sentences. I didn't know this at the time but I was connecting sounds to letters and learned from pictures, symbols, and patterns.

I also really loved my godmother. Her name was Doña Panchita. She and her husband were from Puerto Rico. She was a devout Catholic and a soft delightful person. A short petite woman with black hair and some gold around her tooth. I would eagerly wait to see her when she visited. She always brought something for me or had kind words to say. I had a very strong bond with her. Whenever I would see her enter our kitchen, I would jump off of my brother-in-law's lap or stop doing whatever I was doing and rush to her. My godmother would always kiss me and give me a lot of attention. Her kind affectionate words and graceful smile would make my day. I had the best Godmother ever.

· · · · ·

My parents knew a farmer who would bring fresh fruits and vegetables to our house. He was a tall man of Hungarian heritage with a lazy eye. He always had work clothes on and a baseball cap. He'd come in and stand in the kitchen with his back up against the counters and talk to the grownups there with a cigar in his mouth. I never saw him being paid but I am sure he was. He was the only source through which we got produce. One day, I was upstairs chatting with Rosey when she asked me to get an apple from his truck. The truck was parked on a dirt road in front of our house. It was the parking spot of most people who visited us. I went outside to the truck, climbed up stepping on the rear bumper of the old gray primered Ford, and managed to get in the back where the fruit was stored. I grabbed the largest apple I could find and jumped outside.

I held the apple with both hands behind my waist and walked through the kitchen, hoping no one could see what I was hiding behind my back. As I went past, everyone saw the apple and smiled with a laugh. The farmer asked me with a chuckle if it was all I had taken. I nodded in agreement. Everyone in the kitchen laughed as I made my way through the kitchen and upstairs to my sister. I gave Rosey the apple and said, *They saw me.* She just laughed.

Back then, we frequently had adults visiting from the old country. My parents were also known as people who belonged to the old country. The visitors were all friendly. Any person who came over would talk to me and play around with me. It was nice to be surrounded by friendly people who gave me attention. I loved their company whether they were at our home or we were at theirs.

One of the people we visited most often was Tia Tiola. Tia Tiola was a very short Aztec Indian lady from Mexico. When my aunt went to Mexico to get my mother, she came back with two of the older six children born there. They lived with Tia Tiola until my mother and father returned to the states with the other four kids. Dora was one and an older brother, Roy, who lived with Tia Tiola until my parents returned with the rest of the family. Tia Tiola had an emotionless face and was about 4'9", with a bow leg that caused her to waddle as she walked. Her flat feet fell out of her flat shoes on both sides. She had dusty colored, long, thick, black-gray braids wrapped around her head. She had a beautiful little garden in the backyard where she planted fruits and vegetables. Whenever we went to Tia Tiola's house I would always go in the backyard and pick apples. She also had a swing on her front porch and we kids would take turns riding it. It was my favorite thing about the house. There was a joke that she was somebody who went to everyone's funeral despite being a hundred and one years old. That also included funerals of people who were older than her! I used to think she was everybody's Tia.

Across from Tia Tiola's house lived an older Mexican lady that wore a dark knit wool stocking cap in July. She'd wear dark clothes and a dark sweater. She was medium height and thin. She'd walk around and talk to trees. She acquired the nick name of "Uga Buga." I never did know what her real name was. Most children were afraid of her and if they had to walk past her house, they'd step out into the street and walk around her house. Once passed, they'd come back up onto the sidewalk. To this day, my family still calls stocking caps, "Uga Buga" caps. They're quite fashionable today.

The other house we visited very often was Doña Lara. She was a Mexican lady who lived with her husband, Tereque, above a Pick-n-Pay shoe store. Doña Lara had a habit of hiding her money in the oven. My mother used to say, *"If she ever forgot the money in there, she might burn it up someday."* We usually visited Doña Lara on holidays, and she would cook us some delicious eggnog. Dona Lara was a short, stout, peculiar lady that followed a person around with her eyes and an expressionless face that had the look of fear. My mother told me she often thought that people were looking at her through the windows and how she was afraid to stay home alone at night because they might do something to her.

I have great memories of my parent's house. I spent the formative years of my life there. Once, my older brother, Joe, brought his wife to our house. She sat on the chair where Marie's husband, Heller always sat. Running through the house, I entered the kitchen and saw her sitting there. I immediately went to her and tried to climb up on her lap just like I did when Heller was seated in that spot. I was unable to climb up and I kept slipping down.

The only way I could get there was through her help which was not offered. My brother saw my efforts and told his wife, *"She wants to sit on your lap."* She helped me get up and placed me on her lap in a rough manner. I sat there, facing the table with folded hands. Both of us sat there silently. She did not speak a word, nor did she share a smile. I believe I was three years old at that time. I got down and went away. They say little kids can sense if something is not right, and it turned out they were getting a divorce that day. My brother, Joe, was one of the older six that was born in Mexico. He moved to northern California after his divorce and had a successful career as an engineer machinist and owned his own business. He did remarry and had four children of his own.

That reminds me of at a time when I was sitting on Heller's lap. He told me that when I want a bottle at night to say to my mother, *"You bitch, get up and get me a bottle."* I don't know how old I was but I did stand up in my crib, that was in my parents room, I threw my empty bottle onto the floor and said, *"You bitch, get up and get me a bottle."* my parents both heard and both laughed. As I was getting older, on another occasion, I took a lipstick out of my mother's Avon attaché bag. My mother used to sell Avon cosmetics so that she could earn more income for the household. The lipstick was inside a white plastic tube and was no more than an inch long. I secretly took it upstairs and applied the red colored lipstick on my lips. I didn't have a mirror and no sense of applying makeup. I hid the lipstick tube under my mattress and then returned downstairs. I stood next to my mother with a proud smile, the smile children have when they want to be considered adults. My mother looked at me and laughed back. I did not have any practice applying makeup and the lipstick was all over my mouth. *"This is how you put lipstick on."* I do not remember using that hidden lipstick again. I don't even remember what happened to it. I was no older than four at that time.

. . . . .

We lived in rural Indiana. It was almost a quarter of a mile walk to the bus stop. We had to walk on the dirt road for over fifteen minutes to get to the stop to take a bus for school. Winters in Indiana are extreme. They are long and freezing. Half the winters the temperature would be below zero. However, springtimes were very pleasant and welcoming. They would bring the warm weather back and that would be a relief, even if the rainstorms were loud and scary.

Lying in my bed at night, the crackling sound of lightning would scare me. The strike of lightning would light up the entire room for a microsecond and I would bury myself in the blanket praying to fall asleep. The sound of thunder would make it even more difficult for me to get to sleep. It would be very silent with only the sound of rain and thunder echoing. The raindrops falling on the roof would sound like gunfire.

In the morning, I would wake up and run downstairs. Hurrying to eat my oatmeal and rush outside the front door. I made my way across the dirt road into a tree thicket. From there I could see the cold water stream the rain left behind. The stream fed into a pond across from it. On the other side of the pond I'd see the wild soft deep purple violets and shiny yellow buttercups that made the scene beautiful. When I was little, that was my happy place. I grabbed onto a limp branch and tiptoed on the larger rocks across the pond to the other side. The branch gave me support and kept me from falling. It felt amazing to be among those violets and buttercups. Sometimes I would even pick some and take them home for my mother. I guess I inherited the love of flowers from her.

I played with my younger brother when the older kids were at school. We would wait for them to return as it was a lot more fun to be around them. We loved watching movies together. One morning, we watched a movie about hobos catching train rides together. Since it was a movie, the hobos always knew where the train was going to stop. So, my little brother and I decided to run away and become hobos. Well, it was mainly my idea, and being the younger one my brother agreed to what I said we should do.

We walked over to my mother who was in the kitchen doing the dishes. Her hair was pulled back as usual in a loose bun. I said, *"Me and Zeek are going to run away and become hobos."*

She glanced at us and in her soft tender voice said, *"Wait."* Mom had a comforting way of talking. It encouraged the listener to agree with her. She went out the back door and returned with two twigs that she had pulled out of a tree. I tapped into her creativity. As my brother and I watched, she spread jelly on saltine crackers and made us finger sandwiches. She picked out two bandanas from the kitchen drawer and placed them on the table. She placed the crackers on the bandanas, brought up the loose ends and tied the bandanas on the end of the twigs. We flung the twigs over our shoulders and were prepared to run away to become hobos. We got as far as the front porch steps and sat down there. We ate our snacks and went back inside. Although this memory is quite simple, it is very close to my heart.

Chapter 4

I was picking up on reading even before I had started school. I started school in first grade. Though they did have kindergarten back then, children were still taken in the first grade at the age of six. My reading skills had made me exceptional and I was taken in on my parent's request.

By the time I started school, I was already dissociated. I wasn't a fun-loving child anymore. I was a lost soul. Darla and I would walk to the bus stop together. She would show me the loops on how to get to school. In winters, waiting for the bus would get torturous. But the moment we would get on the bus, it would feel amazing. The warm temperature of the bus was all that kept us motivated to wait for it. Once on the playground, I sat with my head slightly hanging, facing the ground as I slowly swung. There was a little girl who wanted to play with me, but I was not interested. The girl went to my sister Darla and told her that I wouldn't play with her. Darla came up to me and asked me what was wrong. The only answer I had was *"Nothing. I just don't want to play with anyone."* I just wanted to be alone. I kept on swinging slowly. I remember very little from the first grade. I took a school picture, sat in the front row, gave my teacher a homemade apron for Christmas that she really liked. She told me more than once how her sister-in-law liked it.

Other students appeared to be a blur to me and that went on through all of my school days. None of my classmates seemed real to me. That is what amnesia dissociation is like and I was still stuck in survival mode. The dissociation was much worse when I was younger.

Eventually we moved from the rural area to the west side of town. I became even less interested in playing with anyone as my disassociation was growing worse. I remember wanting to own a purple wall hanging and taking it to our new house when we planned to move. I thought it got lost when we were moving. That was one of my favorite things and I was very disappointed. I can still see it hanging up in our room.

. . . . .

I finished the last two weeks of the first grade at another school after we moved. The summers I just stayed around the house with my mother, walked or rode my bicycle around the neighborhood. Sometimes I'd go to work with ma when she went to clean homes. The second grade was okay. We went to a circus once and I sat next to the teacher. We went to the zoo another time and again I stayed close to the teacher. I remember seeing the electric eel and it actually lit up! I thought that was so amazing. I now look back and think the teacher had me close to her because I was different and a lone little person.

As I grew older and entered third grade, we had a gym teacher by the name of Mr. Bomb. He would look at me inquisitively. His face and eyes are engraved in my memory and I think I will never be able to forget him. He asked me once, *"Gracie, what nationality is your last name?"* I answered that it was Mexican. He reacted to say it wasn't by shaking his head back and forth. He would just keep looking at me all the time.

Another time he asked, *"Did your mother just have another baby? I was looking up on births in the local newspaper and I saw where Yvonne had a baby."* I told him she didn't. *"No, that's my sister."*

Mr. Bomb looked at me in surprise, *"Your sister!"*. Was I the only one in the entire planet who had a sister who was ten years older? I wanted to ask him, but I didn't.

. . . . .

In third grade, I was in a couple of spelling bee challenges. I usually made it into the final rounds. I didn't really know how I did so well, but I guess I was just naturally good at reading and spelling. I was asked to read paragraphs at school most of the time. Even so, I had a difficult time comprehending what I read. I had always had problems with reading comprehensions, at least back then I did. No matter how many times I read a paragraph, it would just be impossible for me to understand it. That's what localized amnesia dissociation does. That part of me was missing or in survival mode. The teachers and my classmates didn't know what to think of me. Everyone made their own assumptions.

· · · · ·

Dissociation was sort of an unknown phenomenon back then, so I was on my own and I was going against the wind. The teachers knew I was different. They didn't seem to care though. Anything that had numbers was a challenge for me. I couldn't put any real thought in anything at school. On math tests, I'd just write a one or two digit number down for an answer and no, that wasn't the correct answer. I'd just make them up. I don't know how the teachers let me get away with that. They just turned a blind eye. I did the same with multiple choice tests. I'd just mark a box, any box. During school, I would mostly be captured in my thoughts, daydreaming with little or no attention to what was being taught in class. I used to sometimes, daydream about being a squirrel living in a cozy tree house. This is what dissociation does. It took my thought process rendering me null and void. Education was not as difficult in those days as it has become now. We would get passed for just showing up. The grades simply did not matter. The grade could be just passing and a student would pass. Back then a "D" would satisfy the state requirements and allow a student to graduate.

I have no recollection of the fourth grade at all. I have a fourth grade school picture so I know I was there. There are no pleasurable memories associated with fifth grade either. My teachers were not happy with me, and I was even slapped once for not being able to put an equation and solution on the board. When I got slapped, I did not tell my parents what had happened. But an African American classmate told her mother. The next day, the mother came to the school, called the teacher out of the classroom and slapped her in the hallway. The slap was so intense that the teacher's glasses flew off her face.

We all heard that. That day I felt significant, although only to a classmate's mother. This was also a time when Civil Rights was in its inception.

President Kennedy was assassinated while I was in the fifth grade. Our teacher broke the news to us that day when we returned from recess. I walked alongside my friend Aileen. I remember the teacher was crying as she told us about the assassination: *"Our president has been shot and died."* I was surprised she had that much feeling. Soon the announcement came over the loudspeaker and we were all sent home early that day. Aileen and I walked home together. We were both quiet and talked about President Kennedy's family hoping nothing had happened to them. We walked home in a somber and quiet mood that day. When I got home, Pa was watching a motorcade on TV tears were rolling down his face. I guess the entire nation was crying at that moment in time. The Vietnam War had also just begun.

· · · · ·

The only thing I remember about sixth grade was my teacher. Besides my teacher, nothing else has stayed in my mind. I started seventh grade in public school. It was the time when I for some reason knew I was lost more than ever. I never wanted to go there mainly because I wasn't learning anything. But it was important for me to get my diploma. That was about my future and I was always optimistic. I'd sometimes have a fleeting thought that this thing that was holding me back was one day going to go away and I'd be okay. I just didn't know when. Our neighbors at the west side went to some Catholic school and I asked my mother if I could join them. I just wanted a way out of the public school. She said I could, and so I did. The classrooms of the Catholic school were smaller. They had combined two grades in a single class there. Seventh and eighth grades were taught in the same classroom and I did both years there. The seventh graders sat facing the south and the eighth graders sat facing the east.

The classrooms were very small, but the time I spent there was more fun than my experience had been at other schools. I don't really remember much else about the Catholic school either. All that I know is I had a great time there. There was Sister Mary Leuegis who really liked me. She would let me ring the bell after recess, which was a signal for the kids to get back inside their respective classes. I would stand on the church porch and ring the big foot long, copper, wooden-handled bell. That sister in particular thought I was very smart. She might have been basing that on my reading and spelling abilities. She talked about me in a kind way after I left the school.

· · · · ·

Pa passed away when I was in the seventh grade. I just turned 13 that year. I eventually went back to public school for the ninth grade. When he passed away, I was neither here nor there on that issue. Just neutral. That is what dissociation is like as it erased all of my emotions. He died during one of his stays and the last one at the sanitarium. My mother told me she visited him a couple of days before he died. He told her that he knew he was going to die because of all the bad things he did to Yvonne. So he knew what he was doing was wrong. He said he had a dream that a nurse dressed in white without a face was beckoning him to come to her. Yvonne died a year before he did. He was quite superstitious. My mother lost the house two years after Pa passed away. I believe she did not want to live there after his death as my mother could have still afforded to stay there. She definitely had the income. This move would be the first of several moves that were to come during my time in high school.

My older brother Joe bought a ranch home in northern California for my mother. He and his father-in-law drove to Indiana to get my mother and us kids. He drove us all the way to northern California with a U-Haul that had our belongings and my mother's spinet piano. We moved into the ranch home from James down to Martin. There were eight of us. Joe's wife and her family were coming over there often as if they lived there too. She would yell at us kids and my mother didn't like that. I don't think Joe's wife liked us. James was recently home from Vietnam when we moved. James and Vaughn returned to Indiana after a couple of months living in northern California. A month after they left, my mother and the rest of us followed. Ma would say that no two women can run the same kitchen. We moved back into our home on Vogue. I think my mother borrowed from her life insurance policy to move back. Darla got married later that year to Jerry, who was also recently home from Vietnam.

He wasn't one of James' friends. I don't know who he knew in the neighborhood. I was actually happy on that day and cried for sheer joy that she'd be leaving the house. Vaughn got married during that year as well and he and his wife Betty moved into a room in our house. I don't think ma liked Betty living there. Actually those two didn't get along. Ma didn't care for her. We lived there for over a year and ma lost that house again. I think Ma did that on purpose. That's how my family is. They don't communicate, they just do things on purpose. Vaughn and Betty went to go live with her mother. Ma and the rest of us kids went to go live in the projects. This was our first time living there. I repeated the ninth grade from a different school that year. Still dissociated and just moving around.

I wasn't getting anything out of my classes. It was very difficult to get through ninth and 10th grade. Dissociation had a profound effect on my school years. When I was in high school, I knew then that I'd be a social worker. To achieve that goal, a diploma was very important. I knew that job was meant for me and I did what I needed to do to graduate. Social work was just starting to really become recognized during this time in the late 60s and early 70s. That's all I knew about it back then too and that it helped people. I wasn't sure what it entailed, just that it was meant for me.

Vaughn worked for the steel plant and bought a house. He had ma and us kids move in with him and Betty. This is the house from where I repeated the 9th grade and a different high school. Ma and Betty already didn't like each other and they were going to live under the same roof where Betty was in control. That was a disaster waiting to happen.

Chapter 5

I met my friend, Ann, in the 10th grade. We spent 10th, 11th, and 12th grades together. She helped me get through high school. She was unlike anyone I had known before. She had long brown hair falling behind her. She was a small person, but very cute, with a creamy complexion and big brown eyes. She wore t-shirts, jeans, and dark brown fringed moccasins. She lived with her family in a cute grey Tudor style home. A lot of boys liked her and girls wanted to be her friend. She was the third runner-up for the yearbook queen, which was for the prettiest girls at our high school. I think comedian Carol Burnett was the one who received the photos and picked the winners.

I was flattered that Ann picked me for a friend. I never knew why it was flattering for me to be friends with her other than it just was. She was very smart, too. To say I was terrified at the beginning of our friendship would be an understatement. Being different—and having a difficult time connecting with anyone I encountered—was a problem for me. That's what dissociation is like. I was always thinking Ann wouldn't want to be my friend after she learned I was different and that I didn't have a home. I came to learn that she always had my back and looked out for me. She was a very honest person. She'd say what she saw— the kind of person who would call a spade, a spade and nothing else. She turned into an amazing person and a lifelong friend. She was the closest friend I had. Having more trust in her than my own family is what eventually came out of our friendship.

Ann wanted to be a nun and teach English diction. She was Catholic and went to a Catholic grammar school before I met her in public high school. I believe she felt bad for me for not having both parents or a home. She always watched out for me and only wanted the best for me. She was really concerned about the responsibilities I had to deal with in life. I was living life alone, abandoned by my family. and paying my own living expenses at such a young age. She worried about my nutrition and whether I had enough to eat. She didn't like my sisters and mentioned that more than once. If it wasn't for her, I would never have made it out of high school.

Other acquaintances I met growing up did not wait around for me like Ann did. Her father liked me a lot too. Ann had other friends. Out of all of them, her father told her that he loved me. When I met him, I was afraid of him knowing my background. I was afraid that he'd tell Ann to not be my friend. I am glad I was unnecessarily worried.

Ann's father was a man of short stature, with short wavy thick black hair which was usually combed back. He had a very dark complexion. Whenever I saw him, he would be sitting on the couch, sunk in his deep thoughts, leaning over, with his fingers running through his hair. He'd look up at me and smile. Ann's mother was of Polish heritage. She was always in the kitchen cooking, sautéing onions, garlic, and dill for her perogies. Her father was very proud of his old country heritage. He was from Czechoslovakia. In their house, you could see old framed art on the fireplace mantel and knickknacks placed about. Both Ann and her father were excellent judges of character. Eventually they both became significant to me. The only thing that ended our friendship was her death in 2018. Ann will stay in my heart forever.

· · · · ·

I liked the other young people I knew from high school, but our interactions were different. If they'd take time to come over and talk to me, I just agreed with what they said, and shied away from them as quickly as I possibly could. It felt as though they were invading my space. I wanted to talk to them, but I couldn't. I never had much to say and had a difficult time articulating my feelings. For me, life was like driving on a highway or freeway. I was just driving along, taking the turns without thinking and I'd just get there.

I was standoffish to them because I was afraid of them knowing that I was different and didn't have a home. I knew if any one of them was around, they wouldn't let anything happen to me. Someone being mean to me would have angered the whole high school. Back then, I never knew this directly. Rhonda, a girl in my homeroom, once said to me, *"You have a lot of 'slack' in this school, Graci."* That's how I knew that *"slack"* was a slang word used back then to describe when people were willing to protect you. I eventually knew because Rhonda told me. I was quite surprised to know that. I thought everyone knew I was different and didn't really want to be around me. Knowing I had slack made me feel even more different.

Not having a home of our own during this time, we were living with my older brother, Vaughn, and his wife. He worked for the steel plant too. That living situation made me feel even more out of place. My family was not the typical family other kids from school had. The school I attended was an upper middle-class school. Most of the kids lived with both parents and even had their own rooms. I had a make-a-room that was just off the living room. with a dark brown hard plastic accordion door that pulled shut and shared a double bed with Carolyn. Martin slept on the couch, Zeek shared an open den with ma. My older brother Doug had the only and second room upstairs. He had the door. Vaughn and his wife had the biggest room upstairs. If I had any feelings during my dissociated time, my living situation made me feel very uncomfortable. I had a fear that if others found out, I would be even more exposed. I always felt inferior to the typical student and these complex feelings, combined with my disassociation, made life quite difficult and all my older sisters did was heckle me and say mean things to me and expose me any way they could. Because they didn't think I'd ever remember that night.

I had a difficult time comprehending what I read. I never told anybody about that throughout my school life. I wasn't sure I had a problem, but I just knew I couldn't get anything out of what I read. No one ever said anything to me either. I don't know what they thought. Darla was the only one who made mean comments to me. Darla would say, in a snapping and condescending way, *"Graci doesn't know what she reads."* She'd say that for others to here, no matter who they were. She was always looking for an opportunity to bully me.

I never saw Darla bring books home or take books to school. I never saw her reading a book or studying for a test. I think she knew just enough to be dangerous. When I would face difficulty in a class, she would say I shouldn't have taken the class. Deep down I always knew I would shine being a social worker one day, and despite all the negativity thrown at me, I still believed I'd manage and that was something I had to do.

Every now and then I did something surprising. In my high school public-speaking class, I read a biography of Louis Braille. He was the man who invented the braille reading system for the blind. For some reason, I was able to comprehend that story, and actually managed to give an oral book report on it. I came through on that one! I don't know what happened, but I did a fine job. I would also have a real life encounter with the Brail later in life. I did that one more time when I gave a speech on STDs. I even went to the Department of Health and got STD brochures to pass out in class. That one was important because it was the 1970's. Those were two rare and unusual occasions. I didn't realize what I had just done. That never happened again. Not back then.

I tried to do other speech assignments but just couldn't. They'd just let me decline to participate. No one would say anything to me. I wanted out of that class so badly. The written portion of the Braille report ended up on a small stack of materials that was being submitted to the National Honor Society. I really don't know what happened. There was always a part of me that knew I could do well in academics and one day that part would shine through. That part of me was just non-functional during my time in Indiana and around my family. Through all my school years, no one ever talked to me or asked me anything. Schools were filled with educators, but I wondered if they even cared at all.

Chapter 6

I still wonder how the educators I came across never knew what was wrong with me. I received no help from any teacher. There was only one teacher in the 12th grade who inquired about me. He asked my friend Ann what was wrong with me. He was picking up on something. That year was 1972 and women's liberation was really taking form and gaining momentum. During that year, Ann and I took the first half of the semester in home economics. The second part of that semester we went to auto mechanics class. Mr. Durke was the teacher. He had us work on lawn mower motors. We learned how to give a car a basic tune up, change a tire, check the oil, and do other basic mechanical tasks to keep a car running. Whenever I see a light on in my car, I still think of Mr. Durke. He said those are "dummy lights." Back then, there might have been at least one light in our car that would light up. Ann had an old 1960 Ford car with a cowbell hanging on the rearview mirror. When we'd go over a bump, that bell would make an awful clangy noise. Sometimes, we'd sneak out of school and go to a fast food stand for lunch. She didn't like going to the cafeteria and I was with her.

Mr. Durke was a short man with short black thinning hair combed back. He had an olive complexion and soft brown eyes. He wore a white lab coat and was usually wiping his hands with an auto towel. He had a sensitivity about him. During class I would look up at him sometimes and catch him looking at me intensely. I smiled and he'd return the smile. My head would go back down immediately after that. When he'd smile at me, I assumed he knew there was something wrong. At least his eyes were not cold like Mr. Bomb.

He once saw Ann in the hall and asked, *"Ann, what's wrong with Graci?"*

"I don't know if anything is wrong with her," Ann replied.

"Why is she so skinny?" Mr. Durke treated me with much care and appeared to like me. He cared a lot about his students.

Ann explained my routine to Mr. Durke, *"Graci told me she goes home after school and goes to sleep. She just forgets to eat."* I slept a lot back in those days to avoid what was going on around me.

She wasn't wrong. I would bathe and go back to bed for the night. This was my routine on most days. I would also not have to interact with my sisters. On Sundays my mother made her homemade spaghetti dinner. My sisters all came over. While the oregano and sauce were simmering, my mother was browning stuffed meatballs with long stem onions and breadcrumbs on the stove. She'd smash a meatball for me and pour sauce on it. She'd hand that to me on a little platter. I loved when she'd do that. It was like a little treat just for me. After eating that, I'd go lie down. I didn't enjoy my sisters' company or the world around me.

I am just a naturally thin person. My mother once said to me, when I was in high school, *"Graci, I know you're skinny and you don't like it but just wait until you get older."* I wasn't sure what she meant. I never really gained much weight. I like it now. I didn't back then, though. I would often sleep to avoid doing something or doing nothing. I preferred this routine All through school, I kept thinking I would try harder, and the next year I'd shine through. During my school days, that next year never came. Sometimes I thought I just wasn't trying. I didn't realize I was unable to. That was because of the dissociation of which I was unaware and the toxicity my family brought. I maintained staying in survival mode to deal with their continuous crushing blow insults.

· · · · ·

In the early '70s, Ann and I went to a couple of house parties. House parties were really big back then. People were hanging around smoking pot and listening to the favored rock music of the time. Neither of us was really into drugs. When we'd go to a house party, we'd take a hit off a joint and sip wine. I didn't like doing that and Ann didn't either. We didn't want to be perceived as narcs though. So, we'd take a hit or two. We only did that a couple of times. I really didn't pay much attention to who was at the party. I just wanted out. Space was too confined. As long as I was with Ann, I felt safe.

I didn't like getting high. I was already disconnected and didn't need any help with that. Drugs just made me feel really weird. I once ate a half dozen glazed donuts after I got high from pot. I knew that couldn't be healthy. I also tried cocaine two times. The first time doesn't count because I sneezed, and the coke went all over. It tickled my nose. I just lifted my head and looked at the young man across from me. The young man's house I was at started licking everything he thought the cocaine was on. When I told my friend Richard about this, he said, *"That must have been his cocaine."* It was. That was just funny. So I thought. Never again after that. My heart started racing too fast and that scared me. That was my bout with drugs. Drugs were really big in the '70s. Everyone I knew did them. Most of the young adults thought they had the answer to everything. They were just going around high from what I know. Everyone is so different now and have really cleaned up their acts a long time ago.

· · · · ·

Just before I finished high school, my mother bought a used car. It was a '67 Chrysler. The car was for me to get her to appointments and take her places. I knew my sisters were not pleased with this arrangement. After I finished high school, I started working for a large discount department store as a cashier. I made $1.85 an hour and thought that was so good. This store was equivalent to Walmart and in a nearby town. I had just turned 19 that summer in June. The weather was warm outside.

I loved being around my co-workers and the customers. Even though I still didn't talk much, I enjoyed being there and was happy. I would go on breaks by myself and sit alone. I didn't know anyone there and nobody knew me. All the employees were nice to me and that place gave me a lot of hours to work. Working there was like being in another world. My mean sisters weren't around to make me uncomfortable. The hiring manager really liked me too. She would, at times, give me a lot of hours to work. I would have long lines of customers at my register. I was happy there and did really enjoy that job.

I came home one evening to find my mother waiting for me in the kitchen. As I pushed open the screen door, she was standing there with her hair pulled up in a bun and her apron on. She looked at me and said, *"Vaughn is selling the house and we have to move."*

She continued pretending she was not hurt by my brother's decisions. *"I asked him if I could rent the house. And…he said no…. He…he didn't want the headaches."*

. . . . .

I felt so bad for my mother that day, probably the same way she felt for me. She knew I was tired of moving. She was already on a limited income with Social Security. Then she had to worry about moving. She still had four of us kids in her household. We were given a one month notice to leave. Within a month we moved out into another place. I was still working at the store and had no stress of being at a dysfunctional home.

I had my work schedule up on the refrigerator for my mother. Dora was visiting our home when I was at work, so I wasn't there to meet her. It had probably been a month since we had moved into the new place. This was the second brief time that we lived in the projects. One evening I came home early. I noticed a U-Haul truck pulled up all the way to the front door. I was scared. I ran inside to get to my mother. As I entered through the front door, I saw that all our family members were there. They were taking away our personal belongings. Dora spearheaded that move.

Dora was running through our home grabbing anything she could take. She didn't stop until our home was empty. She took everything but my bedroom set. She was leaving that behind to be mean. Like saying, here's an empty home with your bed in it. I stayed at my mother's side. My body felt weak. Dora was going through our coat closet and said to me, *"We're sending you guys to Harold in San Diego and we're sending Ma and Carolyn first."* My mother was sitting right there and said to me, *"I want you to come with me."* I said to Dora, *"Ma just said she wants me to go with her."* Dora just turned her head like she didn't hear and continued grabbing our things out of the closet. When Dora was having ma's piano lifted out of the apartment, my mother softly said to me, *"Look what they're doing to my piano."* I couldn't stop them. I only cared about my mother and didn't think of anything but her. I told ma, *"Once we get settled in somewhere, they'll send that to us."* She said, *"No, they're not going to give that back to us anymore."* My legs wanted to fold and collapse.

I, with my mother and younger three siblings, then went to stay with my sister, Marie, until we left for California that same year. It was all arranged by Dora. My brain had shut down. For me, life was coming to an end. I wasn't going to have my mother or the younger kids with me anymore. My older brother, Doug, took the car we had. It was hard to get my family to care about anyone or anything. In fact, that proved to be a hopeless cause.

My sisters capitalized on my dissociation and well, they weren't the only ones. My mother and my niece, Carolyn, were the first ones to leave for San Diego before the rest of us left. Carolyn was a little taller than me. She was cute and had thick black curly hair. I always thought she was smart and had a good vocabulary. My little brother turned into a tall young man. He was of big stature with thick black curly hair. He was disabled due to the polio he contracted when he was two years old. It left him crippled. His right arm was affected and he walked with a limp. Most of his right side was dysfunctional. My nephew was only nine at the time. He was quite sensitive and caring. He was also smart and had developed an interest in music at an early age.

· · · · ·

For me, 19 (my age) did not turn out to be a good number. Fall approached and took me off guard. I had no idea what was lying ahead of me that fall. We were uprooted once again and sent to San Diego. We left two weeks after my mother and Carolyn had gone. I continued moving around like I was driving on that highway not thinking and I'd just get there. Upon arrival at the San Diego airport, my oldest brother's wife, Carmen, was there to receive us. I was coming down the escalator with my little brother and nephew when I saw her. The sun was shining brightly, conflicting the darkness of the sorrows accumulating inside me. My stomach felt like it had a big knot inside. It was the point at which Carmen broke the news. She said, *"Graci, the doctors say that your mother has an organic brain disease."* My legs felt weak. I wanted to fall. I tenuously held myself together. I just wanted to get to my mother.

We got to my brother's house where I was led to a bedroom. It was the bedroom that my mother and I were to share. I put my suitcase down and looked around. There was a double bed and dresser in the room. My brother and sister-in-law's room was directly across the hallway. I was still feeling weak. My brother had a large home with four bedrooms and two baths. He worked for the shipyards and had a successful career with them. His wife, Carmen, worked for a sewing factory. They had 10 kids of their own from 5 years old to 21. Standing on a little hill in his front yard, you can look south and see the lights of Tijuana, Mexico from there. My oldest brother Harold, was one of the older six that lived in Mexico. My mother was in the hospital. I asked if someone could give me a ride to go see her. I was taken to a hospital where there were people with behavioral and cognitive issues.

In the hospital, there were patients all over. I was led to a unit. The door had to be unlocked for me to enter. It was locked again once I was inside. I was hoping to find my mother. When I walked in, I saw patients wandering aimlessly along the corridor. I was led to where my mother was standing. I walked over to her and held back my tears. I held onto her arm as we walked.

We sat down on a bench in the hospital lobby. An older patient was sitting next to my mother and said in Spanish, "Debe preocuparse mucho por ti para visitarte acqui`." "She must really care about you to visit you here." My mother translated that for me. I knew my mother didn't belong in that hospital, but I was helpless. My older brother had all the control and he was listening to Dora. I went back to Harold's house. On the drive back my mind was constantly telling me that I was all alone. I was quiet the whole ride. When we reached my brother's house, I went inside and sat on the bed without saying a word. Not knowing where life was to go from there. I missed my mother so much and felt alone and helpless. I fell back on the bed and went to sleep.

My mother came home to my brother's house a couple of days later. She was using a cane. She could barely speak anymore. Her speech was now affected from what ailed her. I lay next to her in case she needed anything and cared for her the best I knew how. Bathing her, combing her hair, and taking her for walks were my daily routine. Knowing more about care-taking then would have helped me immensely. I did my best.

One night as we were lying asleep, my mother began to nudge me on the side. I awoke and asked her if she needed to go to the bathroom. She kept nervously nudging me and wanted to say something. I now know that she knew something was about to happen. I got up and took her to the bathroom. I sat her down when she started shaking uncontrollably. I got scared and called for my brother. He came in and helped me to get her back into bed. She was having a seizure! We called the paramedics who came and took her to the hospital.

After a couple of days, I went to see her in the hospital. I was so lost and didn't think of the situation we were in. I knew it was bad though. Ma came home a couple of days later in a wheelchair. She was lying in bed one quiet afternoon when I heard the phone ringing. I ran into my brother's bedroom to get the phone. The doctor was on the other end. He told me that after running tests on my mother, they had found a brain tumor.

My mother was diagnosed with brain cancer and the doctors only gave her three more months to live. It was September. After I hung up, I fell to my knees and began crying. I was begging God to allow my mother to get well and live. I called Dora's house in Indiana to let her know and to tell other family members. Now I know that doing so was just giving her a heads up. I was dissociated and mostly unaware of my immediate surroundings. Dora wanted the rest of whatever was left of our belongings. She really made sure I was down and out with nothing. She later did go back and take my bedroom set too.

Within three weeks of that phone call to Indiana, the family arrived at my brother's home. They actually made life worse for my mother and us kids. No one really cared. They were only concerned about their own lives. Rosey was kind of a mean person. With age and time, she became meaner. She said she wanted to go back to Indiana. *"I'm not ruining Christmas for my kids."*

Darla was about 24 during that time. She was quiet and hardly ever spoke. She'd stand around and just listen to others. She lacked scruples when it came to eavesdropping. She's still like that today. She said she wanted to get back because her husband said he was getting lonely. That was her first husband Jerry. Marie wore her black hair in her beehive and was quiet. She didn't say much. She was always quick to anger. She wanted to fight everybody. I think because all she's been through made her edgy like that. My brothers acted like they were on a vacation. They wanted to go to Tijuana, Mexico. No one cared that we were losing our mother. If they did, they sure didn't show it!

Dora always wanted to be the center of attention. She was probably in her 30s at that time. She was walking all around the house. She didn't make direct eye contact with anyone. She'd just stand there talking into the air. She talked lightly as if she was happy. She appeared happy to be there. She spoke gaily and with a sly pirate smile. I remember her saying, *"I got all of Ma's and the family's belongings. I got everything."* She was referring to our personal belongings. She got the loot and was happy it had been given to her. In reality she stole those belongings. She was actually happy about that. My mother was too sick to stop her and she took advantage of that and my dissociation.

Dora just stood around where there were people and acted like she was in charge. When in reality all she did was make a big mess out of an already bad situation. My brother had his ten kids and now, we were now there. I'm sure that's just what the doctor ordered for him. Dora ran into the bedroom where my mother was lying down.

She started going through the closet saying, *"I'm going through the closet and taking all of Ma's clothes. They'll fit my sister-in-law back in Indiana."*

It was as if she was robbing a gravesite. My mother was lying right there and could hear her words. It must be awful to not have empathy. Dora, on the other hand, was gladly grabbing everything she could take.

Dora went to the living room where people were gathered. She stood there and gladly blamed others for my mother's downfall. She spoke with pleasure in her voice, *"Ma never had anything."* She said, *"Ma wanted me to have her belongings. Everything was given to me."* It was the only fake emotion she'd ever show. She'd say things like, *"Finally, Graci doesn't have anyone anymore."* As if her day had come. She'd say that I was too spoiled and nobody wanted me around. By doing what she was doing, she was giving the impression that she was the matriarch now. Darla just followed her around like a puppy. The last time I saw them in 2008, they were both still like that. The elders just let them get away with that too. Of course, I don't think they saw things as I did. I wouldn't be at all surprised to learn that others in my family are dissociated. I just kept my distance. Being dissociated, and not really being present in the moment, I'd hear and see things, I just didn't flinch.

They all left after two weeks. My sisters had a myriad of problems in their own families. Dora and Darla watched other people and talked about them, neglecting their own families. They criticized others too. They'd bounce back in their own messy families they made and praise them with glory and there was plenty wrong. That's where their problem lay. It never ceased to exist either. That's their story.

My aunt, my mother's baby sister, came to the house after most of my siblings left. She continued to care for my mother. My brother gave my aunt full control over the situation. My aunt enjoyed helping her sister. One could tell she sincerely wanted to help. My aunt was a very caring person and marched to the beat of her own drum. My aunt had her oldest daughter with her. She told me to leave with her daughter when her daughter went back to their home in Los Angeles.

· · · · ·

My mother died that December. I left and missed my mother dearly. She was all I had left, and she had protected me. I had to come in terms with reality and accept the fact that I was to live the rest of my life without her. I don't think that ever did hit me. I think that just eased up with time and grew old with me. I was a lonely nineteen-year-old who had no one to look up to. I didn't know my journey was going to be such a long perilous one. I travelled this journey alone. When I left my brother's house in San Diego, I had no home, no job, no mother, and just thirty dollars. I had to make the money last. That winter I grabbed my suitcase and left for L.A. hoping for a new beginning.

Part 2

My Disassociation

Chapter 7

A person suffering from dissociative localized amnesia loses her self-iden-tity, reasoning, logic, perception, judgment, and emotions. My thought process was gone. I also had a very difficult time remembering faces. The only way I'd remember them is if that person forced themselves into my life, in-tentionally or unintentionally, and remained a constant. There are several dif-ferent types of amnesia and different causes. I'm writing about amnesia that is not of a physiological nature but of a psychological one. The three most com-mon types of amnesia are Localized, Selective, and Generalized amnesia. My localized amnesia lasted for over three decades and left me in a state of not knowing who I was. I knew my name, age, and who my family members were. This I knew before I dissociated. That is about the only part of my life that stayed with me and continuing to live like this with no help wasn't going to be easy. I forgot all about the traumatic event that took place. Even Though, it was there, stored away deep in my memory, I could not recall that event. Not living around my family. All three dissociative disorders are brought on by trauma. I'm writing about the one I experienced, localized amnesia, and I'm writing about my case only and my experience. "Localized," a thematic and traumatic event, is either witnessed or endured causing the sudden onset of amnesia and can last minutes, days, weeks, months, and in rare cases, years. "Selective" is when a person forgets only some of the events during a certain time period or only parts of a trauma. "Generalized" is when important auto-biographical information about themselves—their name, family, or friends are

forgotten. There is another one, "Fugue," a person can have generalized amnesia and be left in a state of bewilderment and wondering. They might take
on a new identity. Some might even forget a learned skill they once had. I'm
sure there are instances where they overlap one another. There is also dissociative identity disorder (DID), formerly known as multiple personality disorder. That one is different from the others. These disorders are brought on
by either witnessing and enduring a trauma of one or more thematic events.
I'm writing only about the dissociation I experienced—dissociative localized
amnesia. I am referring to my case only as we have different experiences. Based
on a small sample from a small community study conducted by Stanford University in 2019, researchers found this disorder, dissociation, affects about 1%
of men and 2.6% of women. This particular disorder often goes undetected.
More research is needed on this topic with a more extensive population. The
doctor told me, during one of my therapy sessions, that emotions are a very
big part of dissociation. That was after I told him that I once prayed to have
feelings. That was in 1986 and the night I left Indiana and knew I wasn't returning anymore. It was as if I was dead from the inside. A person cannot function being dissociated. In any given situation my body would be in the present;
my mind would simply be absent. I was disconnected from myself. When I
was younger I had no concept of the world around me.

The doctor told me when a person dissociates they usually come back
right about the same time. Mine was a rare case as it lasted for over three decades. He asked, with glee and excitement in his voice, how I had made it this
far? He said, *"You got far."* He thought that holding a post grad social work degree is really raising the bar. He was so impressed. I just smiled and continued
to explain my life. I think, because I read a lot and look everything up helped
me immensely. Not to mention I left my family behind and didn't have their
dysfunction around me as a constant. Not living in Arizona I didn't. I pretty
much schooled myself as I was getting older. I'm a lifelong learner. I'd describe
myself as an autodidact person and I wouldn't give up on myself. I had to believe in myself and that I'd get over whatever was holding me back.

No one knew I was dissociated. Most people thought I just wasn't paying
attention. Being dissociated had a profound effect on my learning capability.
I had to have tenacity and patience. I just couldn't perform tasks. I was empty

without a thought process. My intellectual thought process just wasn't there. Whether it was school or jobs, all of them were affected. I would try really hard, but my situation never improved. Sometimes I even questioned my existence. There was nothing my conscience could relate to, as if I was to live in this world all alone, even without myself. I made many mistakes. Some of the same ones over again and again. I just wasn't getting anything out of life. Being dissociated, I encountered a number of misfortunes in my life. I grew into a stunningly beautiful girl without a soul.

· · · · ·

During the late spring of 1959, we moved from the rural area to the west side of town. The weather was warm outside. We moved into a house on Vogue Avenue. It was a big yellow house. My life from elementary school to the early teen years was spent in this house. It had three floors, a large kitchen, a dining room, a living room, and a small den. My mother kept her piano in the den. There was a banister that led upstairs to three bedrooms. There was the girls' room that had two full-size beds and a twin bed. There was a boys' room with two sets of bunk beds. The floors were all parched hardwood or had very old thin grey carpeting.

Our parent's room was the smallest room upstairs. Of course, there was a bathroom. There was an upstairs door at the end of the hallway that led out to a balcony. In the basement, Pa had a workshop set up for himself. That's where he went and drank his beer. There were wooden shelves in his workshop, and that's where my mother kept all of her canned fruits and vegetables. Rosey married the same year we moved into the house on Vogue. There were eight of us kids left at that home including the two grandchildren, Carolyn and Martin. I have always considered them my younger sister and littlest brother.

One summer evening, I joined Pa and Ma who were sitting on the front porch. Pa asked me, *"What do you want to be when you grow up?"*

I replied, *"A cleaning lady."* My parents laughed and I smiled.

He asked again, *"What do you want to be when you grow up?"*

The second time, I said, *"I want to be a teacher."*

I must have been about eleven. Pa made a school room for me to play with down in the basement. It was complete with a blackboard, teacher's desk, and chairs. Playing school, with some neighbor kids and me as the teacher, was fun. I would write 1 to 200 on the blackboard and then point at it with a yard-stick. Pa sat in the background as an observer. He was quite partial to me. He also made a jumping rope for me. He cut a long piece of rope and looped the two ends that he used black tape to hold the loops. That also identified that it was *my* jumping rope.

The other kids knew he was nice to me and I sensed them not liking it. He was partial to me because I knew his secret, I didn't know this at that time. He was afraid of me for that. The doctor pointed that out for me. He said, *"He never did anything to you because he was afraid of you."* He had every right to be. I would have told someone that cared. When he wasn't home, Darla would really turn up the bullying on me.

When I was about seven, I was reading a book to my little brother. We were in my parent's room sitting on the floor. The door was locked. As we ate raw cabbage with salt and looked at the pictures, Darla began to knock hard on the door.

Mean and demanding like she always was, she said, *"Open this door!"*

I replied, *"No, I'm reading to Zeek."*

Darla aggressively demanded with a harder knock, *"Open this door, I'll tear your book."*

"I'm really not opening the door now. You said you'd tear my book."

She responded in a calmer voice, *"Open the door—I won't tear your book."*

I was sitting on the floor and jumped up to open the door holding the book open in one hand. She slapped the book out of my hand. It fell on the floor. She picked it up and angrily tore it in half. She threw it on the floor and stood there with her arms crossed angrily glaring at me. Her look said, *what are you going to do?* I saw Dora sanding right behind her. I picked up my book and cried.

Darla was a mean girl and she's still a mean person. It's sad that I don't have many fond memories of her. I liked playing jacks with her. Even that only happened a few times. We played Old Maid cards another time. She taught me how to double dutch jump rope. Then she stopped playing that with me. She didn't want me to know or learn anything. My older sisters never wanted me around. They would sneak off and do things without me. They'd tell me later about the fun they had. I really didn't care. I suppose if I hadn't been dissociated I would have felt hurt. At any given time, I couldn't say where any of my brothers were. They were outside from the moment they got up in the morning. They were outdoors young men. They enjoyed camping, fishing, or playing in the woods somewhere. When they were older, they could almost always be found at the pier fishing.

Our father died in 1965 when James was in Vietnam. He was pulled out of a foxhole and sent home for thirty days for Pa's funeral. The following day, after James arrived home, there was a big write up in the local paper where an entire troop was ambushed in Vietnam and there were no survivors. That was the foxhole and troop James was in. I've said, the Grace of God pulled him out of there and sent him home. I was sitting on the basement steps listening to ma when she started shaking out his army fatigues. She said, *"Look, Vietnam dirt."* He went back after thirty days but didn't return to his army buddies in the foxhole. I used to follow James around as much as I could. That stems back to childhood days. He talked to me and told me scary stories. When I was very little, I'd follow him down the dirt roads. He'd hear the pitter patter of little feet and the name James being called out. Sure enough, it was me.

When James got back from Vietnam, his army friends would come over. The ones that were lucky to make it back, including James. I'd play cards with one of his army friends. Mac was a very tall 6'2" thin man with short, straight black hair that had just enough wave up front. He wore black horn rim glasses. Even though he was good looking , he looked like he just walked out of a 1950's high school yearbook. He taught me how to play blackjack/21. We'd play and he'd let me win all of his quarters. I must have been about 13 because our father had recently died. Who would have thought, Darla decided she wanted that particular army buddy for a boyfriend. She was about 18 at the time. She told me once that she thought he had the bluest eyes and they looked like water. I didn't even know she was paying attention or how she got him to ask her out for a date. That's how much she watched what I was doing and Marie said she was sneaky. It sure appeared that way. After he took her out on one date to an amusement park, he came over the next day to visit. She ran downstairs and sat next to him on the couch. I came in through the front door and saw them sitting there. I was on my way into the kitchen where ma was frying chicken. I stopped short as he started saying something to me. I saw Darla nudge him with her elbow and say tell her. In a deep mean loud voice he said how they saw something that reminded them of me at the amusement park. He said they saw an ostrich with skinny legs that reminded them of me. That was so unexpected and out of character of him to say that to me. For a split second that one actually hurt my feelings. I would have never expected him to say something like that to me. I can just imagine how their date went. They walked around and all Darla did was talk about me. That's Darla! I used to call her rickets back then, which wasn't nice of me, because she had really skinny legs with big knees. I saw a picture of that in ma's medical book. She never did forget that and didn't let that go of that either. After Mac said that, he got up and hurriedly walked out of the front door. Darla ran back upstairs. He never came back to our house after that. I wish she would have never done that. He sure didn't like doing that for her. I didn't see him again until I ran into him when I was 23. I stopped at a store one night after work and saw him. I walked up to him and said hi to him. I wasn't afraid of him. We talked for a short time. I still didn't have much to say. We went to a restaurant to get something to eat and had a coffee. He walked me out to my car and opened the car door for me and closed it. He was just a gentleman. He made good on the ostrich remark. James got married when I was in the 8th grade. He and his wife moved in with us. I don't think ma liked her. Ma still had a relationship with his old girlfriend. Those two really got along well. She'd come over and visit ma when James was in Vietnam. Both her and her mother visited ma then. Ma adored that girl.

Our house was a simple one, nothing extravagant. We had what we needed. Pa overcompensated me and went out of his way and character to be nice to me. I had a carte blanche with him. He never was much for words with me or anyone else. He hardly ever said anything. He would only talk to my mother and sometimes me. The older kids were never around when he was at home. They'd just take off and go to a friend's house. Darla just stayed upstairs in the bedroom looking at herself in a mirror applying cover girl make-up. She'd practice facial expressions in the mirror too. As far as I know, she's still like that today. .She used to remind me of Snow White and the magic mirror.

Pa worked between different plants at the steel plant. He told me once that he had a bicycle at work that looked like mine and he'd ride that between plants at the steel plant. I thought that it was nice that he had a bike at work. I was growing, getting older, and knew more. Every two weeks when he would get paid he would look for me. He would give me an allowance of 50 cents, and I would run to the candy store down the block. I wanted my little brother to have an allowance too. I started having him come with me to meet Pa on payday. Pa would give us both an allowance. We would run to the candy store. When Pa would come home at 3:00 pm, he would leave his lunch box out on the kitchen counter. I would see it, run over, and open it up. He would save me half of his snowball cupcake as a treat. He would stand in the background with a smile on his face. He would watch me open the lunch box and get the cupcake.

None of the older kids were usually around when Pa was home. When they knew it was almost time for Pa to get home from work, they would scat and were nowhere to be found. I was told he would whip the kids with belts and sometimes with the buckle. He would take them in the basement of the house and whip them there. Another time he grabbed a hose outside and started beating one of my older sisters with it until her nose bled. Stupid Dora was standing around watching. I never saw any of that. He'd grab anything he could and arbitrarily hit one of the kids until they were well bruised. I was told all of this later in life. If we'd go places with our father and mother, all of the kids would pile up in the back of the station wagon. If anyone looked inside they'd be seen piled up on top of each other, sitting on each other's lap and real quiet. Not making a sound. No one wanted to sit next to him. I was always the last one to get in and would sit between Pa and Ma. I didn't learn, until years later, how much of a tyrannical father he was. I always sensed that something wasn't good between the other kids and him. I just didn't know what that was. He hid the tyrant side of himself from me. I would have either tried to stop him from hitting the kids or told on him. I was like that. I never wanted to see them hurt. I also think that my mother began to use me as her weapon against what he was doing to the kids. She'd often say, *"Graci isn't afraid of anything, she'll go right up to a person and start talking to them."* That wasn't me being fearless. That was dissociation. I was more like, I didn't give much thought about anyone or anything. I was invisible. Learning about his tyrannical side after he died, from the older kids, is only because I asked. None of that surprised me. That was the tension I sensed. Years after he died is when I learned that he smoked. The family still doesn't like to talk about our home life. Unless it's about putting me down. I think they finally stopped that though. That was only because I figured out what they were doing to me all along and told someone that cared. If his name is brought up, it's usually a favorable anecdote. They were still trying to find some way to respect him. There is strength in numbers. There were eight of us kids. We could have taken him a long time ago and lived a much more peaceful life. I would have spearheaded that move.

Even dissociated, I developed a strong bond with my siblings. From the kids I grew up around, that bond was never returned to me. I didn't want to see them get hurt and I wanted them to have things too. Our home was more like a closed lip. No one talked to anyone unless it was something important. That's what life at our house was like. Where one would hope to get encouragement, there was discouragement and strife. If hope was needed, there was despair. Tearful emotions meant a person was feeling sorry for him/herself. Crying wasn't an emotion to be displayed at our home, no matter how badly a person felt. A person was considered strong if they sucked it up and put on a brave face. Affection was never seen in our home. Whatever was normal for a supportive family was not in evidence at our home. I was dissociated all this time because of the secret and the family toxicity. However, it had its way of making me stay blissful.

A neighbor girl started her period and told me about it. Her mother came over to tell my mother about it. My mother turned to me and said, *"Graci, did you come sick yet."* she was asking me if I started my period. I didn't at that moment. I did a short time later. I was thirteen and when I went to get a Kotex from the box in our bedroom closet, I thought, how do I use the belt. I was able to get one on a Kotex belt. I don't think I ever did that right either but it worked. It stayed on the belt. That was a process in itself. In our house, we just had to go figure. The human physiological anatomy or how the body works just wasn't discussed or even brought up in our home. None of that was ever talked about in our home. When I first saw a Kotex box I was about 12. I thought there was a bride doll in the box, wondering who is getting a bride doll. The box was lavender with a picture of a young lady in a brides' gown and veil. When I looked inside I saw what was inside that box. I wasn't quite sure what that was, but it didn't look interesting. No one in our home ever talked much about anything and that never changed. Because of the non-verbal communication with the dirty mean stares, and them thinking I wasn't paying attention, I just didn't think to ask. If I ever did question anything, I'd get a mean answer and the others would just laugh. My sister's would deride and laugh at me if I asked a question. How pathetic.

· · · · ·

My hometown was dubbed the "melting pot city." There were many different cultures, and heritages from the old country. People came there because of the factories and there were several. Most of the kids I knew had their fathers working at one of the major factories, be it the steel plant industry, shipyards, or the Ford Motor Company. When I was eight years old, a little boy from around the block liked me. We liked each other. Craig was of Irish heritage and was also eight years old. He'd ride his bicycle past my house.

One day, I was standing at the end of our driveway by an old oak tree stump. Craig rode his bike up to me and stopped. He held out his hand. His hand was in a little fist with something inside. When I placed my hand under his fist, he opened his hand and sparkling amethyst jewelry fell into my hand. He then rode off on his bike. I took the jewelry into the house, upstairs to the bedroom, and placed the pieces in a drawer. I recently found an old music sheet of my mother's, faded pink with calligraphy written black letters that reads, "Sweet Lady of Seven or Eight." There is an elegant gentleman in a black suit with groomed short black hair sitting down in a chair crossed leg with an open book and a dandelion in his hand on an open page. I have that old music sheet framed in my home today. Reminds me of the innocence and Craig.

That jewelry turned up missing. I think Darla was doing something with my favorite things. She was always keeping an eye on who was around me and what I was doing. That eventually turned into an unhealthy obsession. My favorite things would almost always turn up missing. I didn't pay much attention to my favorite things then. I realized this as I look back in retrospect. This would go on throughout my life until Darla married and moved out of the house. The first time she married she was about 19 and married Jerry. He was quite handsome. About 5'9" medium build with a tan complexion and green eyes. He was. nice to me Darla didn't like that, but he didn't care. I don't know why he got married. He sure wasn't ready for that. I was actually happy when she got married and moved out. That still wasn't my happy ending with her. She carried on with her abusive behavior. She tried to get Jerry to team up with her to say and do mean things to me. He wouldn't do it. He told me she was jealous of me. Not in those exact words but he did tell me. Her life was too much consumed with my life and what I achieved or was trying to achieve..

· · · · ·

When I was nine years old, Pa entered me into a pageant. He was a member of the Mexican American's Citizens Club (MACC). The MACC was holding a fiesta and five girls were entered in the contest. I remember my mother measuring me over and over for my dress. She had taken me to a lady's house that lived on the south side of town. This lady was making all the girls' dresses for the fiesta. Pa would wait outside in the station wagon. My mother and I would go in through a side door and down some steps to a dark, dingy, musty smelling, cement basement. The basement was lit by only one light bulb hanging on a wire from the ceiling. I would walk over to an ironing board and get measured once more at this lady's house.

I came in as fourth runner up at the pageant. There were a lot of children and parents present at that fiesta. My yellow dress was floor-length and that required me to wear a wire can-can underneath to hold the dress out. My sisters, Marie and Yvonne, were getting me ready for the fiesta. All the time they were primping me, they were saying how this was making others feel left out. None of us knew that I was dissociated and being in the pageant was neither here nor there to me. When we completed the stage presence of that night, I walked off stage and up into the bleachers where Pa was sitting. I sat down next to him and don't remember any more. I just knew I was invisible and no one could see me anyway. That's what dissociation does. Nothing seems real. It was a beautiful colorful fiesta filled with old country heritage. Being able to appreciate the fiesta wasn't going to happen, not while I was disassociated. With dissociation, you can remember some things.

Other things that are related to memory are often irretrievable. I might have appreciated that event more if I wasn't dissociated. To this day, an old acquaintance will mention something about me from the past and I just don't remember the specific incident. For instance, I was recently talking to an older acquaintance from the steel plant. She was telling me that I took her to go visit an older nephew and wife who just had a baby. That's pretty significant and I don't remember that at all. I had to be in my middle to late 20s. The baby was premature at six months gestation but she made it! However, being born into an already dysfunctional family, with Dora as her grandmother, didn't help. This older acquaintance was always good for lifting my spirits. She started telling me of some things that happened to people she knew. She also said, *"Who just picks up and moves to another state where she doesn't know anybody?"* A dissociated person in search of the self was my answer! I recently read a quote, "A year ago I did not know today. I didn't know how I'd make it here. By grace I made it here." If someone would have told me back then where I'd be today and the way my life turned out, I would have believed them. I just wouldn't have known when. And I met a cast of characters along the way.

Two years, after the fiesta, I was up in the attic and found that same big yellow fiesta dress. I tried it on to learn if it was still a good fit. I went downstairs to show the dress to my mother. She was in the kitchen standing by the cupboards. If I wasn't dissociated, I would have been surprised to see Darla up and downstairs sitting at the table. That was a rare occasion. She hardly ever left her room. She acquired the nickname of "bags" for that. She was presumed to be sleeping up there. Her eyes were baggy. In reality, she was avoiding Pa. He had recently died when Darla was sitting at the kitchen table talking to my mother.

I said, *"Ma, it still fits!"* She looked at me and didn't say anything. My family wasn't much for communication.

Darla looked at me and began to yell. *"Throw that dress away!"* She added, *"That's all dirty on the bottom,"* while angrily snapping at me.

I was so scared that I took the dress off and actually threw it away. As I was stuffing it into the garbage, Darla continued to yell at me pointing at the bottom of that dress, *"Throw that away, it's all dirty on the bottom!"* *"It's all dirty on the bottom!"*

She was a mean girl growing up and thought only of herself. Darla would growl and bully me just about every time she saw me. She is still like that today.

My mother (as usual) never said a word. I know my mother didn't talk much. But if she was asked a question, she would answer. I know she did answer me. The kids were just not accustomed to speaking. So, no one asked her much of anything, if at all. We all just silently moved around or the older ones would say mean put downs to each other or me if I was around.

After Pa died, I'd go up to bed at night and Darla would pretend to be sleeping. As I'd get into bed, she'd sit up and turn her head toward me and say, *"I'm going to hit you."* Then she'd start punching me in my arms, one after the other. She looked like a boxer in a trance-like state punching his training bags sweating profusely. Only the punching bags were my arms. This went off and on for about two weeks. I would cry, *"Stop hitting me. I'm going to tell on you!"* She punched really hard and always made me cry. Once my little niece Carolyn was present and got caught in the crossfire and was hit too. Telling on Darla would have gotten her into big trouble and I didn't want to do that. Until one night she punched me in my upper arm. That pain radiated through my whole arm, down into my fingertips. That one sent me running downstairs and I cried to my mother, *"Darla has to stop punching me in my arms!"* That's when she finally stopped.

I know Pa spoke nicely to my mother at home. He never argued or showed anger toward her. He never raised his voice to her as far as I knew. But he also didn't do anything for her in the way of gifts or taking her out somewhere. That he did by, and for, himself. The older girls would say that he was selfish. It certainly appeared that way. My mother continued to clean houses after he died. I didn't like getting up and going downstairs when she left for work early in the morning. That house was lonely and scary without her. I didn't trust my sisters either. They were all mean to me. They wouldn't say or do anything to me if my mother was there. If my mother wasn't there, I was most likely to be victimized.

I don't remember feeling anything over Pa's death. I sensed that the older kids, who were still at home, were neither here nor there on that issue. I think my mother was glad that the fear was over. Mother used to say she would never remarry. She would say that she wouldn't have another man boss her around. She told me once that she admired Jackie Kennedy because she advocated for women. I believed her.

We lived in the house on Vogue for two more years after Pa died. During that time, Vaughn got married and he and his wife moved into a room in our house. My mother eventually stopped making payments on our home. I don't think she liked Vaughn's wife living there. Wherever we lived after that, she had to pay more for rent than our mortgage. Waking up and going downstairs when she left for work early in the morning made me feel alone and scared.

I was very close to my mother. Never wanting her out of sight where I couldn't see her. She was my safety net and the only constant in my life. Following her wherever she would go if I could. She was kind, soft-spoken, and a friendly person. Everyone that met her liked her. I thought she was really nice to other people's kids. She would babysit for people too. The kids she babysat loved her. They would tell me how much they loved her. A neighbor's girl described her as an angel. She would always be around the house with a dress below the knee and an apron tied around her waist. She was either cleaning, cooking, sewing, or playing her piano. She had an angelic way about her. When I think of her, the only word that comes to my mind is *softness*. She had beautiful delicate hands with porcelain-like fingers. Her hair was either pulled back in a loose bun or she would have a hairnet on. She always made sure our home was clean. She had an indulgent parenting style. I think that was because our father was cruel, mean, and strict to us; therefore she turned around and gave us liberty. She allowed the kids to come and go as they pleased. There were no set times for anything. I really don't think she would have married my father if she knew what he was like before they married. They married and he hurriedly whisked her off to Mexico. That's where she found out what he was like.

Chapter 8

The summer weather was warm in 1972. High school was finished for me and I started working as a cashier at the department store. In the fall, my mother became very ill. She complained of headaches. She started to lose her balance on one side. Her gross motor skills were being affected. I didn't know what was wrong with her. She was often quiet and spoke less than she used to. She would sit in a chair with her head in her hand. In those moments I was helpless. None of my mean sisters would come around much than either to help. We left that fall for California to go live with my oldest brother, Harold. My sisters in Indiana didn't want to be bothered with caring for our mother. She also still had four kids at home.

It was a beautiful warm Indiana Indian summer when we finally left for San Diego. I cared for my mother there. I did the best I could. Shortly thereafter, she became a total invalid. She passed away that December in '72, just two weeks before Christmas. We, the remaining kids, were farmed out. My older brother in Northern California took my little brother and the two grandkids my mother was caring for. By then Carolyn was 14 and Martin was 9. I went back to my hometown in Indiana, and stayed with Darla. Darla told me to go back to Indiana and live with her and her husband, Jerry. After I got there, no one wanted anything to do with helping me. They enjoyed running around saying that I didn't have anyone or a home. Dora actually enjoyed saying that. The others enjoyed hearing her say that and that it was actually true. Life was just going to get harder and for years to come. I just played my hand as the cards were dealt from the moment I awoke throughout the day, until I fell asleep at night. That's what living with amnesia dissociation does to a person when their own family couldn't give a damn.

· · · · ·

Once I took a history class from a local community college in my hometown. It was one of the first college classes I took. It was probably in the early 1980s. I still remember how the professor once asked me how long I had been in the United States and I had no answer. Not knowing how to answer that, I just gave a blank stare and became invisible. Using the blank stare was common behavior for me. That and thinking no one could see me anyway. I would then wish a person would stop talking to me altogether. It was only a matter of time before I had to drop that class because I was unable to comprehend the professor. My entire life was quite distressing.

Keeping to myself and living alone was normal for me. Not wanting to go places where I would have to interact with people was typical for me. The thought of socializing made me feel very uncomfortable. During those years if I went anywhere, I always went with Ann. I didn't have the confidence to be alone where I had to interact with people. Most of the people I met thought I was shy and different. Some people found me to be an interesting person.

A lot of times I felt ashamed because I didn't have a home or normal family. I don't think anyone knew how I was to be approached. Telling someone of my dysfunctional family wouldn't have been believed. When people would approach me, I would feel suffocated as if I couldn't breathe. All I could think of was to escape. Many people perceived me as meek or a pushover. Whenever I had to walk in a crowded area, I'd look down. I didn't want anyone to come and talk to me. It was kind of a signal that the company wasn't welcomed. Oftentimes I'd have fleeting thoughts of how I wanted to be perceived by others. Those thoughts changed rapidly. My own family, mainly my sisters, would belittle and expose anything about me every chance they'd get. I sure didn't trust them. I knew they didn't like me, not really. How could they when they didn't like themselves. The part of themself that they did not want to bring to light.

. . . . .

The year was 1972 when I went back to Indiana and started living with Darla, and her first husband Jerry. She was quiet and didn't say much, at least not to me. Her husband was living like he was single. He was dating some of the girls I remembered from high school.

The first job I had was working for a printing company in my hometown. Darla knew a girl that worked there and got me in. I don't know why. She eventually turned against me there too. She was making a mess out of whatever I was doing. There was absolutely no encouragement coming from my family. Darla gave me rides to work during that time. It wasn't far from where she lived. We were mainly printing brochures. Work slowed down after about six months and I was laid off. I just waited and hoped to get called back. It was going on six months and other employees that started work after me were being called back and I wasn't. I decided to apply for unemployment. Soon after I applied for unemployment, the printing company called me back. I was told they tried but couldn't get a hold of me. I didn't know why. They had my phone number and I was always home. Whatever the reason was, I was happy to be back at work and making a living again. I was able to get a new car with no down payment or co-signer. In the evenings, after Ann and I left a club, we'd go to a popular restaurant known to young adults. We were eating breakfast very early one morning when two men from a modeling agency approached me. They gave me their card and asked me to contact them. I always thought that would be nice and I would have liked to do that and wanted to. I never followed up though. Being dissociated, that was never going to happen. That was one of my dreams unfulfilled.

. . . . .

Being dissociated, I did not have a concept of the world we live in. I was living in my bubble and that bubble included nobody else but me. In my early twenties, I had started living alone. Listening to a lot of music kept me going. I was unaware that the music was about real-life experiences. Experiences that most artists encountered in their lives. I just liked listening without thinking much about the lyrics and artists. Once listening to a Bruce Springsteen song, I read its lyrics and was mesmerized by them. I thought he was really smart and found his lyrics to be really abstract and well-written. But I was unable to comprehend them. That song was from his *Greetings from Asbury Park, N.J.* album. I think the song was "Blinded by the Light."

Another time I was having a conversation with an older nephew of mine. He was talking about a Lynyrd Skynyrd song. I forget which one. When making a comment about that song, my nephew said in amusement that what I said was exactly what happened to them. That is when a light bulb lit up in my mind and music really started to hit me. That reminds me of a time when I was about ten years old. Sitting on my neighbor's porch, remembering my neighbor telling me that her mother was afraid for her oldest brother who might get drafted into the war. Surprised to hear about the war, I asked her what war she was talking about. I did not know there was a war going on. Waving my arms around I said, *"There is no war—just look."* It was the time of the Vietnam War. I was so unaware of what was happening in the world.

Chapter 9

There were problems in Darla's marriage. I moved in with my older sister, Rosey. Eventually, I had enough to pay for a crash course in keypunching from a local business college. I attended night classes for three weeks. I knew that keypunch operators at the steel plant were paid well. I did have to support myself and thought that would be good employment for me. The owner of the business college was teaching the course. She talked to me one night and asked me if I was having a hard time understanding lectures. Nodding in agreement, I quietly said yes. That was the dissociation. I didn't know that then. I did get through that course. At the end of the course, they would hand out certificates with how many keystrokes a person could punch without any regard to accuracy. That worked in my favor.

· · · · ·

One day Rosey's husband said to me, with her standing there, that a friend from his work saw me. His friend asked him how he could stand having a girl that looked like me living in the same home. I knew that was the beginning of the end to that living arrangement. I wanted the floor to open up and swallow me. I was having a hard-enough time trying to live somewhere. Rosey started having marital problems and asked me to move out. After about a month, she yelled at me and told me to move. She wasn't a friendly person. Knowing I had nowhere to go, she gave me four days to find a place to live. She was mean and yelled a lot. She didn't talk; she just yelled. She's still like that.

From her living room, one evening, she said, *"Graci—get something to eat."*

I opened the oven and saw what was there to eat. I replied, *"There's chicken in the oven."*

I went to get a piece of chicken out of the oven. I reached in, but there was thick black hair wrapped all around the chicken leg. I threw that piece back in the oven on the tray. That made me sick. I wasn't hungry anymore. Thinking about that piece of chicken on and off throughout life, I know she purposely did that to me. She knew I opened the oven door and didn't eat anything that night. The week before I moved from her home, I could get no hot water to take a shower with. It turned out that she was turning the hot water off on me. It was wintertime in Indiana. I had to go to my older brother Doug's house to take a bath. It was painful.

I called Darla and asked her if I could move back in. She told me she had to ask Jerry. I followed up with her the next day. She still hadn't asked him. I waited another day and it was the same. After the third day, she told me that Jerry had said *"no."* With one day left to find a place to live, I eventually grabbed my small flowered suitcase and moved in with some hippies that knew about my plight and offered to let me stay with them. I slept on a mattress on the floor in a bedroom there. I kept my suitcase close to me as it contained all of my personal belongings.

I didn't want Ann to know how and where I was living. I didn't want to say my family wouldn't help me. To me that was embarrassing and would expose the family I was born into. I thought no one would believe me anyway and I would have been ashamed to tell that to anyone. I pretended as they cared. I would just go out to meet her. Unbeknownst to me, she followed me one day. One evening, I heard a knock on the door. I answered it and Ann was standing there with another friend. She asked me to come outside to talk. She told me she spoke to my brother Doug and he told her I could live with him. I hurriedly went to the room I slept in, rolled up whatever was mine, grabbed my blue suitcase, and out the door I went. I moved in with Doug and his wife that I remembered from high school. He helped me a lot by offering me a place to live during those trying times. I slept so well that night.

. . . . .

I found a new job over 60 miles from my hometown. The job was keypunching for an automotive warehouse. Making $2.30 an hour was barely enough for survival. My only motivation was hoping I'd gain some experience after working there for a year. I didn't know anyone there and no one knew me. I still couldn't keypunch. Everyone there was so nice to me. Sometimes I'd think they felt sorry for me being alone in this world. Traveling so far to get to and from work was tiring. During my stint at the automotive warehouse is when I moved from my brother's home into my first apartment. That was only one apartment down from my brother's.

When I got my first apartment, furnishing it wasn't easy. I bought a brown tin entertainment center for $5 from a neighbor who was throwing it out. I went to "dollar day" sales at a local discount store and got kitchen and cleaning supplies from there. I bought a bed for $28 from Goodwill. I bought a TV for $125 from the auto warehouse where I worked. Rosey gave me a 1960s round table, clock, lamp, and electric coffee pot. I bought a sofa for $30. That was funny. It had brown and gold stripes with four thin wooden legs. I found that in a newspaper classified ad. That was it.

I eventually applied to a hospital in my hometown for a job as a keypunch operator in their billing department. My boss from the automotive warehouse had given me a good reference to the hospital. I ended up working there. That was much closer to my home. I started on the second shift there. I wanted those hours, so I didn't have to actually work with anybody. The hours were from 4pm to 12am and I worked there alone. The pay was $2.10 back then. I knew that was less than I had been paid at the automotive warehouse, but the job was a lot closer to home and much easier on gas, too. Of course, I lacked the confidence to work there or anywhere. Walking into the billing department, while the day shift was still there, I would often hope no one would look at me. I'd walk in with my eyes down and go over to a little room where the computer was. No one else was in the computer room.

One afternoon, I walked in and there was an employee sitting in an office to my right. He said "*hi*" to me. I didn't answer and cast my eyes down. I didn't want him talking to me. He was very offended by that. He stayed late some-times and sneaked around to the computer room. He peeked in to see if I was in there. One night he asked me what I was doing. Using a calculator, I ex-plained I was *"running a total on some billing."*

Another evening towards the end of my shift, after everyone was gone, I put my head down on the desk. I actually fell asleep. He walked into the computer room and shook me. He reported that. I realized that not re-sponding to his "hi" really got to him. Just trying to live my life dissociated was an arduous task.

I was relieved when everyone left at 5 pm. I didn't know any of the girls and there were a lot of them. Some of them I had gone to school with. I didn't know who they were while in school or in that billing department. I didn't even realize this until I left that place and started living in another state. My friend, Ann, ended up working there as a switchboard operator. Since they had a lot of employee information, the girls in that billing department knew who I was from school as the shy, scared girl who didn't pay attention.

People perceived me as somebody who lived in her own world and they weren't completely wrong. In fact, they were almost right. I couldn't perceive much of anything since I was dissociated. Now I feel like I am the eye in the sky. The only thing I regret is wasting most of my younger life. No one knew what to say or do. I do know that I had a lot of protection from my peers. That goes all the way back to my school days. Most of my peers looked out for me, including in high school and life after that. I didn't like that though as that made me feel even more different.

I had difficulties with relationships. That was mostly because the emo-tional part of me wasn't there. I had a very strong friendship with a young man when I was in my twenties. That lasted for about five years. It could have be-come a long-term relationship, perhaps even marriage, if I could have con-nected with him on an emotional level, which I was unable to. I wanted to fall in love and be emotionally connected to someone, but disassociation never al-lowed me to. Not being there emotionally had a really bad effect on any situ-ation I was in. I am somewhat surprised to have survived those difficult years for as long as I did in Indiana. I absolutely had no help from my family. I was better off not asking for any help from them. They'd just laugh at me having to do without. All they ever did was pull me down. All through my life, I'd get two steps ahead, they'd find out and put me ten steps back and with a vengeance. That's just how my sisters are. Especially Dora and Darla.

Chapter 10

After a year at the hospital, I finally had my chance to apply for work at the steel plant. This was in my early twenties. I was actually 23 at that time. When they called me to take a keypunch proficiency test I was happy and nervous. Most of the employees there were all generational. That place was run by World War II veterans and family connections were important there. Lacking confidence, I didn't pass the keypunch proficiency test. That really disappointed me.

For some reason, I was lucky, and they hired me anyway. That was unheard of. The steel plant was ultimately where I wanted to work because the pay was $6.50 an hour. Knowing that salary could support me, I was happy. Eventually, I became really good at keypunching from working there. My shift was from 3pm to 11pm. Eventually, I worked a swing shift there from 7am to 3pm, 3pm to 11pm, and 11pm until 7am. I would just come in with my head down and walk over to the data processing building. Most of the time I just sat alone and didn't talk to anyone unless I had to. Soon that was expected. One employee noticed that I didn't talk to her. She was assuming I was jealous of her for some reason. She discussed it with the supervisor who said, "*Oh, Graci is just like that. She doesn't talk much to anyone.*"

In the summer of 1978, Zeek came to Indiana for a visit from California. That was his first time back to our hometown since the dreadful fall of 1972. He didn't like the older sisters either, especially Dora. He communicated to me once that he didn't like what she did to us and ma. He thought she just threw us anywhere among the elements of the earth. He was staying with James. I was going to take him to an Eagles concert in Cleveland one Saturday. The Eagles were his heroes. They were playing a concert in Cleveland. There were five of us going. That was on a Saturday night. On Friday before, early morning hours, he was hit by a drunk driver and was killed in that accident. All he talked about that Friday before was the Eagles concert. I took his death very hard. I was dissociated, laid down on my couch hugging his picture and cried my eyes out. For some reason, that one really hit me hard.

The work at the steel plant lasted for seven years. It was in 1982 when the layoffs began. That was the beginning to the end of the industrial revolution. After I got laid off, I collected unemployment like the others, and I vacationed in Arizona.

· · · · ·

During my employment at the steel plant is when I met Zachery. He was very handsome and smart. He was about 5'8, petite built, dark complected with shoulder length black hair. He looked like God himself chiseled him. He was a white collar worker at the steel plant. A lot of guys wanted to be like him and a lot of girls had a huge crush on him. I just want to keep his beautiful face frozen in time in my mind. He cared a lot about me and gave me all the encouragement to keep moving on. He once said that he was trying to save my soul. That would have been nice if he could have found it. It wasn't going to happen with Dora and Darla around. He knew something wasn't quite right with me.. Knowing I was alone in this world, he tried to protect me as best he could. Then I had both Zachery and Ann.

If I could have emotionally connected, he would have been "the one." I didn't have to be around a lot of people with him either. We went on bike rides, talked on the phone, went to a club, attended shows, he'd come over for coffee and knock out the local newspaper's crossword puzzles. You have to have a good vocabulary for those too, talked about movies—well, with me it was more like mentioning a movie—and we generally had a great time to-gether. We were sitting in a restaurant one evening when he looked across the table at me and said with sadness in his words and concerned soft eyes, *"What's taking you so long?"* I didn't answer him. We had a really nice friendship for about five years. He was such a brilliant and nice person. Zachery was also in Vietnam. He volunteered for the draft and worked in medical records there. He was such a smart young man. We both did a lot together. The most I ever did with anyone beside Ann. I desperately wanted to emotionally connect with him but could not. My family was of no help. In fact, Darla was after him for herself, but he wasn't interested. I didn't even know she knew about him. We never talked much unless she was putting me down. Or trying to make me feel bad about myself. That's how obsessed she was with me. She continued to follow me around throughout my life. That's how she found out about Zachery. I never told her. We hardly talked because she would have been of no help. I know Zachery wanted to meet my family as he knew who a couple of them were. I never would do that and I don't think he would've believed me if I said to him that they really don't care about me nor do they like me.

One day Zachery was sitting crossed legged on the floor in a meditative position. He was talking to me and looking right at me. Looking back at him, I thought, *"I know you're looking at me and you're talking to me, but you can't see me."* Running over to the bathroom I looked in the mirror and realized I couldn't see myself either. I didn't know who that was looking back at me. On my birthday, he sent me a card. The card had a picture on it of a loosely connected cow that was clingy. The inside read something about how I was and was not there at the same time. He was smart enough to know something was wrong. He wasn't quite sure what it was though. That card pretty much summed me up. The card was funny. I think I still have that somewhere around my home today. He certainly tried to connect with me.

After he and I drifted apart, it was then I realized that something was very wrong. Anyone else in my place would have been devastated and hurt. I had no feelings about that relationship no matter how hard I tried. Knowing I wanted to care about him more was disappointing for me. Looking at him with no answer because I didn't have anything to say. Knowing we were drifting apart and there was nothing I could do about that. I wasn't really hurt, but there was a sense of discomfort and incompleteness. That alone told me that there was something very wrong. I didn't know that I was locked within myself.

There was another young man that was pursuing me, I must have been about 27. I was out with some people from the steel plant at a club. I met this young man there. His name was Gene. He was gorgeous. Tall, about 6'3", thin, brown hair and blue eyes. A Jr. high school math teacher and basketball coach. He drove a silver corvette and lived in another city. I would have really liked to connect with him but couldn't. The dissociation prevented that. He was persistent too. He'd send me flowers and cards. I knew it wasn't going to go anywhere and I used being rude to him to make him go away. That took a while too. I wouldn't return his calls and was declining dates with him. He wasn't giving up so easily. When I talked to him I eventually told him it wasn't going to work. He told me he was going to go home and cry. When I told the doctor about all of this with Zachery and Eugene, I told him that I cried more than they did. With a sadness in his voice he said, *"Wasn't there anything anyone could to?"* Even if my family could, they wouldn't have. Not for me. They would have just drooled if I took him around them. They'd say something putting me down or expose me uncaringly, hoping they could get him for themselves. That's how they are. They only wanted what I had. Including the men in my life. Later, I realized, Smart good looking men were attracted to me and I was equally attracted to them. Eugene would have realized there was something wrong with me too. I think he actually did and he still cared.

· · · · ·

Being perceived as gay was not surprising. Actually, I had someone come over to me one day and ask me if I was gay. While living in Indiana, a young lady came up to me and said, *"Are you gay? I only see you with that one girl and never a guy."* She was well known in the community to be gay. She appeared to be a very nice young lady. Even when I no longer heard from Ann and lived several states away, that was still a question I heard. Being perceived as gay was nothing new for me. Throughout my life, I've heard that more than once. I am not gay and never was. There's nothing wrong with that. If I were, then I'd say so. However, I'm not.

. . . . .

During my last months in Indiana, I went to go stay with my oldest sister, Marie. I moved out of my last apartment in Indiana and had my personal possessions shipped to Arizona into storage there. March approached and I was glad to be leaving Indiana for good. The year was 1986. The night before I left for Arizona, I prayed and asked God to have feelings as everyone else did. My brother, Doug, bought my car and a morning flight was scheduled for me out of Indiana. If I was going to have to start all over from scratch, it wasn't going to be in the cold weather. I knew then that I'd never return.

During a prior vacation in Phoenix, I met a young lady, Joan. We remained in contact when I went back to Indiana. When I was ready to move to Arizona, she welcomed me to stay with her. Moving in with her was a blessing. Joan was from Nebraska. Her mother had recently died. She left there to get away from the painful memories of her mother. I was connecting to her on that level. She was happy to have me live with her until I figured out what I was going to do with my life. My future was uncertain. I continued to play my hand as the cards were dealt each day. From the moment I awoke, every hour, every minute, every second until the moment I fell asleep. Dissociation consumed every fiber of my being. The following day would be the same. I'm very fortunate to have had fate on my side. My personal belongings were in a storage unit in Phoenix. I had $200 on me and that was it. A little more than the $30 I had in 1972. Nevertheless, I left the cold behind. Loneliness and an inability to organize my life accompanied me. What I was to do with my life remained a mystery. With all this, I was happy to be in Arizona and away from my family. If I was to start over, it would be out of the cold weather. Unbeknownst to me at the time, that decision was one of the best things I ever did for myself. It was a beautiful warm day in March when I awoke to the early morning sunshine of Arizona.

. . . . .

I started working for an employment agency that sent me to the State Department of Revenue. My job was keypunching taxes. The time was early March and taxes season ran through April. I met a friend there. He was working on taxes too. I was on a lunch break sitting alone. I noticed he was also sitting alone as well. I thought he looked like a nice person so I walked over to his table. He started talking to me. I sat down at his table and came to know that he was an artist and his name was Richard. Richard is a tall thin man that has long brown hair in a ponytail, wears glasses and a goatee beard. He reminded me of a throwback hippie. He's still like that today. In fact, he'll consent to being one. I didn't have a car and took the bus to work. The busses stopped running at 11:00PM and I got off work at 12:00AM. He told me he had a car and he'd give me a ride home. This marked the beginning of a great friendship. Fate was once again on my side. When I left for work that day on the bus, I just thought I really needed the money and I'd cross the how I'll get home bridge when I get to it. That's how I lived my life with amnesia dissociation. After a couple of months working with the employment agency, I had enough financially to rent my own studio apartment. I moved from Joan's apartment into my own space. Richard helped me move in and get my items out of storage. We were artistically placing pictures or other wall hangings on the floor leaning them up against the wall. I told him, I'll call this the attic look. He just laughed. We are still great friends to this day.

Eventually, I was hired as a permanent employee by the state. After a short time, I bought a used car from a co-worker. I didn't have to take the bus anymore. Another brave move for me was to transfer over to another state department and work as an eligibility interviewer for family assistance. That broadened my horizons for employment. I wanted to get away from keypunching. That training wasn't easy. I just tried with all my might. Unwilling to give up on myself, I enrolled in classes at a community college. The first time I walked in to enroll, I didn't know what to do. I walked back out. After a couple of months, I tried that again and spoke to a student advisor. It wasn't easy to make an educational plan with him either. I managed to get through that though. Wanting to continue my education has always been my plan. Going to classes and taking classes wasn't easy. Not having my sister's around made that doable and I was willing to take on that battle. Still not knowing I was dissociated, I started taking a couple of classes at that time. Totally unaware if I could do the classes or not, never entered my mind. The dissociation must have slowly begun wearing off when my classes started. With much effort, I was able to get through them. And believe me, I tried with all my might. Every ounce of my energy was brought forth into my classes. There was a lot of time for me to be alone in Arizona. During the holidays, I just kept to myself anyway. That work wasn't easy either. Putting forth my best effort is what I was doing, and my sisters were far away from me. They were out of sight and out of mind. Not for long though.

· · · · ·

Darla eventually came out to visit me. Not knowing what she wanted made me a bit leery, but I obviously didn't ask her that. All she attempted to do was create self-doubt in my mind and how someone told her how pretty she was. I was overly happy when she left. She probably wanted to see what I was doing and how I was managing everything all by myself. I didn't know then that she just wanted to protect her secret. She always only cared about herself. She also wanted to find out what I was doing so she could continue to feed her ego off of me. She is no less than a drug addict looking for their fix. Her fix was upending my life to feed her ego. Dora is like that too. If I had a sister that started with literally nothing, and was doing what I did to maintain her life in a good way, I'd be so proud of her and praise her on how far she was getting. I'd even help her in getting there!

Chapter 11

Meeting my husband through a neighbor was a good thing and a blessing in disguise. Barry is a big man about 6'2 with soft brown eyes and long dark brown hair that he wears in a thick braid falling on his back. I braided it for him. It is short and grey now and he is just as handsome as ever. He has a reddish tanned complexion from living in the desert. He's extremely smart, works with computers, and is a member of the world-renowned super intelligent group MENSA. He had a small house here in the valley. After a few months of us knowing each other, we decided to live together. I was still very happy to be in Arizona. It felt like home to me. It felt so nice and I could finally breathe. Still the thought of getting married never entered my mind. If anything, I knew I'd never get married.

Barry and I married after a couple of years of being together. I felt so safe with him and didn't want to be without him anywhere. I stupidly invited my sisters to our wedding. We had a small wedding in my sister-in-law's backyard. The yard was set up really nice. My future in-laws were really great to both Barry and I and helped us with our wedding. My sisters sat in a back row and all had mean hard disgusted looks on their faces. Carolyn looked really pretty and was my maid of honor. Carolyn's husband and Martin were there too. They looked quite peaceful. After we said our vows and walked back towards the group of people, Darla had her oldest stepdaughter, Karen, with her. Karen is tall, about 5'7 in height, thin, with blue eyes, short permed hair that looks burnt and has a long and pointy nose that just about reaches her upper lip.

They both came up to me. Darla said under her breath, in a muffled condescending voice, but loud enough for me to hear in three hard syllables, *"Fleetwood-Mac."* She was referring to my wedding song which was "Leather and Lace" by Stevie Nicks. Karen gave me an up and down mean stare and said in her muffled voice, *"Where did you dig up that old dress?"* I used a dress Darla wore that she gave to me, years ago, from her second marriage. I cleaned the dress and fixed it to my liking. I liked it and so did Barry.

Dora started in on me saying, *"You are so skinny." "Why are you so skinny?"* Darla chimed in, *"You look like a reed."*

All where no one else could hear them but me.

Rosey just stood there like she did that night. She didn't say a word to stop them.

I think that other members of my family don't stop the bullies or help one another in any way because somewhere they learned helplessness. Their snide, mean comments were meant to hurt my feelings. I was used to them by now and I let their comments just roll off my back. I was still dissociated, but might have had a good start coming out of that by then.

That was my wedding day and they should have been grateful I even invited them. What a mistake that was. They were employing their gaslighting technique and still trying to make me feel bad about myself. They were trying to cast doubt in my mind that I didn't look good and my wedding song wasn't all that. Dora was really pissed off. She wanted Barry for her daughter that had a son and the father didn't want to marry her. That young man was smart not to get mixed up in that family. Her daughter wanted Barry for herself too. Marie told me this and cautioned me not to invite Dora into my home. He surely would never have been interested.

My family is so dysfunctional that they passed that down to their kids. Darla probably wanted Barry for her unmarried and oldest step daughter Karen. That could have been why Karen was so very nasty and mean to me too. I wouldn't be at all surprised to learn that both, Dora and Darla, had private agendas for Barry and didn't tell each other. Those two always wanted what I had, including my boyfriends. Both Dora and Darla reminded me of the fairytale Cinderella. They all stayed in a hotel and I was glad when I knew they left to go back to Indiana. I felt safe again.

. . . . .

The next best thing that happened to me next to Barry was our Melissa. Barry and I decorated the second bedroom just for her. A supervisor of mine at the State Welfare Department gave me a surprise baby shower. I was so moved by what she did. When I walked into the conference room, I started crying. The thought of being important to someone was amazing. No one had ever done anything that nice for me before. I wished that she could be my sister and wondered why my biological sisters weren't like her.

My husband and I put our money together and bought a larger home. Finishing my A.A. degree was my plan. During that time, I went to work for a group home. It still hadn't hit me that I was able, with effort, to complete the classes needed for the A.A. degree. That mission was accomplished! Barry, Melissa, and Richard came to my graduation. My plan was to transfer my credits over to a four-year university program. Most of my community college classes spilled over into the Bachelor of Social Work degree (BSW).

The dissociation had to be wearing off. Still, I was unaware. The classes were difficult for me. Continuing to work in group homes as a behavioral health tech for children, juveniles, and adults synchronized with my studies. I continued all of this while working on my education. I just kept going and didn't give up. Again, wanting to broaden my horizons, I transferred over to the agency's alternative schools and eventually public schools.

I raised a question to the doctor during one of my sessions and asked if dissociation comes off in layers. To my surprise, it did. That memory was buried deep in my mind. I began to develop a very strong emotional bond with Melissa. Melissa triggered that repressed memory and the rest is history. My dissociation was beginning to wear off when my work and school performance began to improve. I owe that all to Barry. He provided a safe environment for me. I was taking on tasks that were once nearly impossible for me to do. Starting to pull in some decent grades at the community college level and receiving my A.A. degree was quite a milestone for me. I was starting to become aware that I was doing things that I always wanted to do but for some reason, I lacked the capability to do them. This was something that couldn't be explained, and

I was only happy with what was occurring in my life. Still unaware of the dissociation, I kept moving on in life.

. . . . .

I enrolled at the university and my A.A. degree classes transferred into the BSW program. The first semester in the BSW program is when I had that first memory flash in my mind. That is the memory where Pa was singing to Darla and me. After that first memory, classes got to the point where I could handle more of them. I became totally unaware of the dissociation or that it was wearing off. Barry was providing the safe, ,supportive environment for me to continue with my education. Our little Melissa joined his efforts in supporting my educational goals. What a team we were during those times. If I could, I would take Melissa to classes with me.

Taking classes in doses, I took two classes to start with in the BSW program. Handling studies and working all the way through was quite challenging. Managing to find time to meet with my study groups was a must. We'd meet at our homes, the library, or restaurants. Being unaware that I was actually doing what I couldn't do before never really occurred to me. With all I was doing and trying to accomplish, I didn't have time to think about that. I just kept going. Studying and working became my way of life. Working as a teacher's aide in the public school gave me insight into what I had missed out on. Our little daughter attended the same school I worked in. Barry and I continued to support Melissa in her school environment as well. Barry is a quiet, calm, and patient man. He has always been there for her too.. She was really strong with music and math. She landed a seat in the gifted classes with her math grades. She plays four instruments. Melissa and Barry got along really well as father and daughter. Her grandmother and aunt on Barry's side of the family gave her a lot of support too. I learned what it is to support a child in their school achievements. Barry came from a family of teachers, psychologists, and engineers. What a blessing he was for me. Melissa never gave us a problem and we are both very pleased with her. She makes us smile. She met a few of my family members but she doesn't really know them and doesn't care either. Life was getting easier for me as time went on.

I was performing tasks I couldn't do before and never really giving any thought about it either. While tutoring some 4th graders in math was when teaching really hit me. I came up with a tool for the students to help them understand percentages. I'm sure it wasn't anything someone else hasn't already thought of. When another student started to help one of her peers, I knew I succeeded with her. A 4th grade teacher that had gifted students in her class, heard me talking to the students making them think. She said, *"That's higher level thinking."* She did ask me for the tool that I came up with. I gave it to her. I really liked her too. My husband, Barry, was a great support for me during this time. I'd put my hand in his. His hands are big, warm, and would easily fit over my hand. That felt nice. My little daughter supported all of my efforts as well. She would always be by my side when she could be. It felt good to have both of them with me. My doctor commented that my husband saved my life. I couldn't agree more. Continuing to chase my dream of higher education had always been my plan. I don't even feel like I was raised with my family in Indiana. I was born into the same family, but other than that, there's nothing there. And that's sad.

· · · · ·

Being at home one night, doing an assignment for the BSW program, I was thinking and writing. Employing my family in Indiana to incorporate the three branches of social work, the micro, macro, and mezzo levels was a blessing. I wrote a part where my mother played the piano and my father would sing. There it was. Like a snapshot flashing in my mind. I saw my father singing to us and Darla's reactions with her crying. Rationalizing what made her cry, made me think that she wasn't feeling well. Maybe she wanted the light off so she could go to sleep? That memory kept coming to me day after day. Like it had a hold of me and wasn't going to leave. Seeing Darla crying, I realized exactly what occurred that night. I told my husband about that piece of memory. I don't think he was sure what to think. I was still unaware that I was dissociated and that particular experience had caused it. The doctor wished I still had that assignment. I turned that in years ago and didn't even think to save it. I do remember it though, the class, and the professor. That professor in particular was a Fulbright scholar from Spain.

The other pieces of that night came to my mind over time without me knowing they had appeared. Not like how the first memory hit me. They just kept coming in until I had all the pieces of that night but one. However, I didn't know I was missing a piece. I saw Rosey and Marie first arrive on the scene that night. They hurriedly walked over to the right side of our bed. They just stood there. Then I saw my mother coming up the stairs. She walked onto the scene and stopped and stood at the bedside. She was where Pa was standing but further away from the bed. Lastly, I saw Dora coming up the stairs onto the scene.

Next, I heard Ma saying, *"We were coming home, and we saw Pa coming down from upstairs. What was he doing up here?"*

That's when Darla threw back the covers and jumped out of bed. She stood to the left of my mother. My mother reached out her left hand and held onto Darla's right hand. Darla was crying hysterically and said, *"Graci kept telling him to stay and sing."* I was doing that. I didn't know anything else was occurring at the same time. Not back then I didn't.

This is where I stood up on the bed with my back against the wall. Beginning to cry, *"I didn't know, I didn't know."*

Looking to my left, Dora was coming at me with an open raised hand, and I heard my mother saying, *"Dora—don't hit her! She didn't know."*

Dora continued to validate Darla by yelling, *"You hear what Darla is saying?"*

· · · · ·

I still didn't know that experience caused me to dissociate. I still think of this scene, trying to make sense of that night and what happened. This scene continued to be a mystery waiting to be solved. All the time, I carried it along. Meanwhile I was handling the college classes and assignments really well. My graduating class refurbished a day care center that was in much needed work. I brought that day care center and the needs to the table in that class. We refurbished it as a class project. My friend Richard painted a child's mural on the day care building. We were all proud of the job we did on that.

I was entering the final home stretch of the BSW program. I had to complete eleven credit hours during the last summer. I needed four more classes.

One was a political science class that required me to visit Nogales, Mexico. This was a three-week course. A lot of my classmates traveled with me. We stayed at a convent with the nuns one night, and another night we stayed with a family in a cardboard house. The house was very sturdy and had sectioned off rooms. Yes, we could stand up inside there. There was not much furniture in there, and what was there was not arranged, but rather dumped. A white fabric curtain served as a door to the bedroom. This was a nice opportunity to learn about Mexican culture, families, schools, nutrition, and *maquiladoras*. We had to write a research paper on those topics.

· · · · ·

On returning from Mexico, I enrolled in three more classes. They started in June and were five weeks long. My grades were really improving, and I received almost all A's. I had only one B. That summer, knocking out the eleven credit hours I needed allowed me to graduate in August. Finally, I was able to graduate with a good grade point average and the BSW degree. Managing to work all the time while studying was a challenge. Nevertheless, getting through that was my goal. By this time my real-life work experience included group homes, alternative schools, public schools, adult education and family literacy. I started working as a teacher's aide in an elementary school that my daughter was attending. That summer, when school was out, I transitioned over to the district's adult education program.

The last summer of the BSW program was difficult especially after working. However, I had fulfilled my mission and was thriving. The university gave me an override to complete my internship. Upon completion of my fieldwork, I received an "A." Working in adult education and family literacy provided me with the opportunity needed for my internship fieldwork. That's what the override was for. I was able to complete that where I worked. Additionally, obtaining my adult education teaching certificate was an incentive. I was a pioneer in working with elementary schools with family literacy engaging parents to work with their school-aged children in the child's learning experience. That was rewarding for me. Both the families and my efforts were featured in a local city newspaper. I was later told, by the assistant principal, that the child's test scores had improved with the parental involvement. After that successful year, family literacy programs started popping up in other schools across the valley. I received a scholarship from the university for my work with the family literacy program. Thoughts of how my parents didn't work with us kids on schoolwork and never questioned us on how we did in school frequently surprised me. Our parents never even asked what classes we were taking or what our favorite subjects were.

My adult education teaching certificate gave me the ability to teach English as a second language. Working directly with individuals and families are some of my fondest memories. There is a section with pictures devoted to those activities in my personal social work performance book. Every picture has a humble story associated with it.

· · · · ·

I never called my family to tell them about my higher education achievements. Or all of the rewarding experiences I was having with employment. My brothers and sisters never would have appreciated it anyway. Darla would have said something along the lines of, *"Who does she think she is. If they only knew her."* I was very happy without them and I didn't want to ruin that by calling them. My educational successes were celebrated with my husband, daughter, and Richard. The three of them, especially Barry, supported me in my latest work accomplishments as well. They were all that I needed. Darla, her husband, and Dora would have tried to cause drama there too. Deriding and attacking my character. Spreading unsavory rumors about me was their dirty game. They really enjoyed doing this and laughed at me too. They'd even put words in my mouth. Some of the things they'd say can only come from a sick person. I've been around Darla long enough to know that she laughs at making a fool out of others. Both she and her husband were laughing at me. He's like her too. Where I don't find any of what they were doing to be entertaining and funny at all. They even got into the department of education. They were awful. They enjoyed tearing down my self-worth in any way possible. That made them look good, I guess. That had a serious, very heavy, emotional effect on me. I knew what they were doing without really knowing. Constantly thinking about what they were saying, and to whom, placed a heavy weight on my mind. That took an emotional toll on me. I'd just pick up on other people's nuances. By what was said to me, I knew who was really talking. That would be Darla, her husband, and Dora. The wording was a big clue.

The emotional effect of what they were doing was like having a very heavy cement brick on my shoulders and there was nothing I would do about that because of who Darla was using to help her do her dirty work. He included himself in on that, too. He's not totally innocent in my opinion. I was beginning to get very ill. Sickly ill. I was having more aches and pains than anyone can imagine. I was hospitalized more than anyone I know for pneumonia, unable to breath, preventable infections, and other sorts of illnesses. I eventually ended up in pain management over what they were doing. Some of the pain I describe as being worse than fibromyalgia. That's how bad it was. I was getting rashes all over, too. There is a saying, As within, As without. That is one I was living to its fullest extent. I think by now we all know that Darla was using her husband the police chief. And there wasn't a damn thing I could do about that. I'll say this again, he's supposed to know what he's doing, too.

· · · · ·

I took a year off after completing my BSW degree. I wasn't sure I wanted to go any further. After that year off, I decided to raise the bar once again and get my master's degree in social work (MSW). I applied to the college of human services at the university and was accepted into their master's program. I was so happy! I had made it into the College of Human Service graduate program. It was one of the hardest tasks, if not the hardest, I ever encountered in my life. Second only to being a mom. In social work, the graduate program is all research and writing. I implemented a medical survey, upon approval, and conducted major research on quality of life and life skills among a specific population. This was my major research paper complete with statistics and theories. I woke up every morning at 3:00 AM to go in the back room and start writing. When I finished that research, turned in my paper, and received my master's degree, I was still waking up at 3:00 AM and a couple of times I actually ran into the back room to start writing when I realized, I'm done with the research paper and graduated already. I'd just hug myself, jump up and down and go back to bed. What a great feeling that was.

Toward the end of the MSW program, I was really racking up the A's. My husband, daughter, and sister-in-law came to my graduation ceremony. It was a smaller graduating class than the BSW. My husband and our daughter clapped for me when my name was called and saw me walk up with my robe and collar on. I had received my master's degree in social work. That was a dream fulfilled and every bit worth it! That I'd do all over again in another life.

Our daughter was still a schoolgirl at that time. My graduation inspired my daughter to seek higher education. A couple of mothers I met during my family literacy days also came to my graduation. They were on campus, asking around, to anyone there, if they knew Graci. Someone did. They were led into the graduation ceremony. I was very pleased to see them. When I looked out into the audience and saw them, I wanted to cry. It was very encouraging. One of the mother's came to my home after the ceremony and took pictures with me. Barry and Melissa gave me a large screen white mac desk top computer as a gift and took me to the Olive Garden for dinner. Richard presented me with an oil painting of Melissa sitting with her cats she rescued from a shelter. I was very pleased.

Chapter 12

During the MSW program, I did an internship with the state as a case manager. I eventually was hired as a result of my internship. I was working as a case manager assessing individuals and families for needed services they were eligible for including domestic violence and prevention. I also was one of the privileged workers that was able to help Hurricane Katrina evacuees. When I was out in the field, I'd go to shelters as well. This was a wraparound service program. I worked with one family that were refugees. The mother went blind and I connected her to a resource that sent her to learn the Brail reading system. I really enjoyed my work as a social worker. I worked in group homes, along with alternative and eventually public schools. I also wrote a successful grant for a school health-based clinic for children. I loved working in the field as a social worker. Those are some of my fondest memories. I loved and enjoyed working with others that were willing to help themselves. I was their hand to hold. I myself was in that very real life situation starting from the very basics and at one time needed a hand to hold. Barry gave me that hand. We all need a hand to hold.

While working as a social worker, I realized that that night had taken me away from myself. I was describing that as, *"I left myself at age four and didn't return for a long time."* I also realized that *"I had to return to myself in order to complete my full circle of life."* I never knew that I was dissociated. It was holding me back from excelling. I just didn't know the cause of the problem holding me back. I wasn't connecting dissociation to my prior life. I had a thought, *"I needed to remember the details of that night to progress in life."* I realized that I left and needed to return to myself to carry on and function as a fully aware individual. I also realized that I had become distanced from myself, and it took a long time for me to come back. I cried over that all night. I still didn't know that condition is a mental disability and is in the *Diagnostic and Statistical Manual of Mental Disorders*, 5th Edition (DSMV).

I told my husband that I needed to talk to someone. I wanted to talk to a professional. I didn't realize that I dissociated at the age of four, over the trauma Pa brought into our room that night. Even though Dora actually caused me to dissociate from fear, ultimately it was Pa that was in our room. What Dora did was a secondary reaction to what Pa did. With the child abuse, in and of itself, he was the source. Dora never liked me even when I was a small child. She felt I got all the attention from our parents, especially my mother, and she was jealous. I think Darla felt that way too. I sure didn't mean to do that.

. . . . .

Growing up, and throughout my life, I never cared about doing things alone. I had anger tantrums. In the second grade I came downstairs wearing a skirt and holding a red sweater. It was a bulky sweater too. I was mad that my mother wasn't downstairs in the kitchen. I started crying, yelling upstairs, asking her to come downstairs. She didn't. I got angry and said to her that I was going to school with my sweater stuffed inside my skirt. I tucked my bulky sweater inside the waist of my skirt and went to school very mad. I was tired and frustrated as part of my dissociation. My mother had a "door mat" style of parenting. I think with all she'd been through and with all the kids, she just didn't care about much anymore. I know she cared a lot about me, though. I just think she didn't know what to do.

. . . . .

I used to like to roller skate. We had a skating arena in my hometown that a lot of kids would go to. I would go there alone. What did I care about. No one could see me, I was invisible. I would rent a pair of skates there and skate around the arena by myself. After Pa died, I went there a lot mostly on weekends. One time I entered a contest there and won a Beach Boys 45 record. My mother would give me a dollar to go skating. Back then, a dollar was enough to get a child in, have him rent skates, and purchase a coke and a hamburger. I just skated around until it was time to leave. I hardly talked to anyone. I couldn't express myself. I did a lot by myself. Most others my age had friends with them at the skating arena, and I didn't. Neither did I care.

I walked by myself to and from school, downtown, church, or wherever else I wanted or needed to go. I literally had no friends. Knowing who a lot of other kids were, them knowing who I was, and being friends are separate things. During my elementary school days, the only friend I had was my neighbor. I never had much to say. I just got used to not talking and being alone. It wasn't by choice but had become my way of life. I didn't like my older sisters around either. I never trusted them. Darla bullied me. Dora showed a lot of anger toward me. She'd stomp her feet and jump up and down whenever she saw me with something new. She did that as an adult too. Especially if I had something new given to me by my mother. It didn't have to be new. Just something my mother gave me. She is very childish. Both Dora and Darla are.

I was in the fourth grade when my mother bought me a necklace with a G on it. I came downstairs and went into the kitchen. Dora was over visiting, sitting at the table. My mother was at the sink. When Dora looked at my necklace, she stomped her feet hard on the floor. Just then my mother turned around. Dora continued to sit quietly and didn't say a word. They all scared me. Especially Dora. Sometimes I found Darla sneaking around a corner listening to who I was talking to or who was talking to me. Those conversations were brief. I never had much to say. I think she is unaware of her unscrupulous behavior. She does that with other people, too. Not just me. In my opinion, I think she is a very disturbed individual.

There was so much I wanted to do but couldn't. I have wanted to model for a long time, since a young girl in high school. When a modeling agency approached me, I never followed up with them. That wasn't going to happen being dissociated. I always knew I wanted to go to college to become a social worker too. It wasn't that I couldn't, but it was the dissociation which disabled me. That was all over the family secret of child abuse and the toxicity it brought with it. My mind and body weren't connected. The latter I did achieve. My time at high school wasn't pleasant. By that time, I was immune to the other kids' snide and mean comments. If I cared at that time, I would have never made it as far as I did in life. I only wish I would have made it here a lot sooner. The dysfunctional family I grew up in didn't help matters either. That's what happens when child abuse is kept a secret. Everyone in my family was affected by our father's behavior. That's why a person like our father cannot stay in the home. The meanness towards me by my older siblings, especially my older sisters didn't help either. Who would think that something as big and severe as what our father was doing would never come to light. It usually does and will. Their secret just kept me in a constant state of dissociation and disabled me. They were mean and bullied me throughout my life and to this day they're still like that, given the chance. My doctor mentioned to me not to expect my siblings to change because they aren't going to. They always laughed and made fun of me. Someone did say to me, *"He who laughs last..."* That was said to me more than once. I forgot who said that to me. I don't think that was meant literally. There's nothing funny about the life I lived. Both Dora and especially Darla have an unhealthy obsession with me. I didn't do anything to them. I didn't care to be around them. I preferred to be by myself. If ever I had a neighbor around, Darla would bully me. She'd try to stop the neighbor from talking to me. All Darla did was tell everyone that I wasn't smart. My schoolwork was never up to the mark and she always told everybody about it. In retrospect, while all this was happening, I realized I had left myself; Hence, returning to myself consumed decades of time and no one gave a damn. That is sad!

Part 3

Mystery Solved

Chapter 13

I never said anything nor talked about myself because I never knew what to say. Nor did I know where to start. I didn't have a home, lived in many different places, went through more than my fair share at an early age, and didn't have anything. That alone made me feel very different. Each day I played my hand as the cards were dealt. I was never able to predict my life or plan a future. Something always told me that the force holding me back would disappear, and that eventually it would be fine. What I did not know was *when* would it all be fine. Most of my life was consumed by dissociation.

Moving on in life and trying to accomplish daily tasks wasn't easy either. Some might have perceived me as being fearless. There was plenty to fear in the world. Being unaware of my surroundings made me vulnerable and an easy target. With dissociation—localized amnesia—I didn't have any sense of how to identify danger.

Once, I was walking out to my car at 3 AM, after leaving a fast food restaurant. I was 22 years old. The place was known for its delicious rib sandwiches. Driving home from work, I had decided to stop there to pick up something to eat. I went inside, placed my order, and returned to my car. I opened my car door and as the light went on, I saw a big man lying on the floor of the back seat. Even then, I wasn't afraid. A sense of danger immediately ran through my mind, but calmness swept over me. I backed up, hurriedly went back into the all-night food restaurant and asked if someone could escort me out to my car. I told them that there was a man inside my car, and I didn't want to go back out alone. The owner knew what was going on and walked me out. That area was not known to be the best part of the town. He gave me the name of the person that was in the back of my car. He said he saw him run off. I knew the name from elementary school and a local junior high school. So that person knew who I was. Others were saying, *"What was she doing out so late at night?"* Blaming the victim was par for the course already.

· · · · ·

When I was living in Indiana, I had family living all around me in close proximity. For example, Dora lived a couple of miles away from me. They never once came to visit me. I never got along with them even if they were in sight. I was always worried about what they were going to blurt out that was mean and derogatory to me that would expose me in a bad light. They really enjoyed doing that. I didn't trust them and kept to myself. Telling a person what I really thought of my family, especially my sisters, wouldn't have been believed and I would have looked like the bad person. I don't think anyone would believe how severe my family dysfunction is. That's how good my sisters were at doing what they do to feed their egos. I think a lot of people in my hometown thought my sisters were some kind of wonderful. Little did they know!

Darla married her second husband in 1975. Robert is a police chief from a really small town. Some people from my hometown referred to that small town as "Mayberry RFD" after the old television show. I remembered Robert being a tall, thick man with brown eyes, and short brown hair worn in a perm. It was a second marriage for both of them and all together they had four children. Three of his and one of hers. They never had any between them because, according to Darla, he didn't want anymore.

She asked me in front of him once, *"What do you think that man in your back seat would have done?"* I knew what she was doing there. Trying to sound smart in front of her husband.

I answered, *"I think he was going to ask me for your phone number so he could ask you out for a date."*

90

Her smile shut down on her face and her excited look turned to a flat expressionless one. I knew I was being a smart ass. My life was sprinkled with men following me home if they'd see me driving somewhere alone.

Another time, I was driving home from work when some man started following me. This was at night after working a 3 to 11 shift at the steel plant. When I pulled up to my apartment, he stopped alongside right behind me so I couldn't back up. He rolled down his window and started saying obscenities to me about what he'd like to do to me. I pressed my hand on the horn hoping for help. Finally, a neighbor above me came out on the balcony. My neighbor was a biker. He just stood there looking while the man rode off at that point. I have been in other dangerous situations, but at that point, I realized I really had no one to care about me. I would feel safe when Ann was around. When she wasn't, there wouldn't be anyone watching out for me. My family couldn't have cared any less about me. I think they wanted me to show up dead. That's because they didn't feel safe with me knowing their secret, plus they despised and loathed me. If anything horrible did happen to me, Dora and Darla would want to get to where I was living to see what I had that they could take. Especially Dora. She'd want to be there first. They'd want to know if I had an insurance policy and who's beneficiary. They wouldn't give me a second thought otherwise. I'm sure that's how they'd think and no one would believe me on how they were after me. I never knew I had the secret they were afraid of either. I don't know how I survived life's perils. Maybe I was destined to live.

Chapter 14

When I left Indiana for good in 1986 is when Ann and I lost contact for many years. I saw her again when I went to Indiana for a visit in 1991. I had Melissa with me and Ann got to meet my little princess then. Ann was so very happy for me that I had Melissa now. She also thought the world of Barry too. Even though she never had the chance to meet him she sensed he was a good soul. We visited for two days and I came back to Arizona.

I didn't talk to her again until 2015. I called her. We talked over the phone for a while and laughed a lot about old times. I could tell she really missed me. I missed her as well. She told me in her next life, she's going to come out to where I am. I'll know if she's around me. Now my lifelong friend is Richard. To this day we remain friends. He has always been there for me and he is someone I can always count on. I tell people that Richard and I knew each other "B.C."—before children and actually marriage.

· · · · ·

Darla and Dora were both employing triangulation. "Triangulation" is where a person will talk to another person about what a third person has said about them. Or going through a second person to get information to a third person. If you look up "narcissist" in the dictionary, Darla falls under that category. Dora does too. They both used triangulation, bullying, projection, arrogance, and gaslighting constantly with me. They'd start with "love bombing"—pretending to care about me—to learn about my social circles so they could make a mess out of my life. Either one of them wanted me to know what they were doing. Good thing I'm smart. I figured this out when I was older. Better late than never! I was always suspicious of them. Never really trusted either one of them. It's sad to be from a family so divided. One would think that they'd get help, but that would be admitting they have a problem. According to them, I'm the only one that had psychological problems. I'm not expecting them to change because I know they're not going to. I'm far away from them and I intend to keep it this way.

· · · · ·

The college foundation coursework at the community college level was hard for me, but I had no intention of giving up on my academics. I was hard on myself. I enrolled in two classes. Eventually, I got through them. I began to take classes in small doses from the community college over the years. I wanted to get away from keypunching and get transferred over to the state's family assistance division. I really wanted to work there. Going through the training wasn't easy. Learning through repetition was the only technique that worked effectively for me.

· · · · ·

When I first found out I was pregnant, I made myself call Darla and tell her that I was having a baby girl. She immediately flew out to Arizona. She said Dora asked her, *"What are you going to visit Gracie for? You have brothers in California that you should go visit instead of wasting your time visiting Graci."* I guess she was trying to trick me into thinking she was loyal.

Darla told me that she told Dora, *"Graci needs me more than anyone else."* She was employing her "love bombing" technique there. Because she is a cold person, she couldn't quite pull that off. Her true self came through. She began to ridicule me asking me how I can do the job I was doing. She kept asking me, *"Can you do that job?"* I didn't know what she meant. I really didn't. I kept asking her what she meant. I don't think she knew either. That conversation went nowhere. She told me she had $50 her mother-in-law gave her for her trip. She was visiting for a week and never once used any of that $50. I drove and paid for everything including trinket souvenirs for her to take back to Indiana. She returned to Indiana with her $50. I was just glad that she left. Darla and Robert are like that. To be frugal is one thing. To be so tight that you squeak when you walk is another. They are known in their hometown for that. I've actually heard that from more than one person. There's nothing wrong with frugality however, people get tired of paying for others. That gets old real fast. They must both feel like they are entitled. I can't help but think they're two of a kind when it comes to bullying and employing their dirty techniques. A later phone call from Rosey revealed that Darla and Robert just bought a ranch home and he paid cash for it. I thought, he has that kind of cash around. He never wanted to pay for anything. Darla either. They were always looking for a free vacation or ride.

I didn't know then that Darla just came out to get some information about me so she could do mean things to me. She didn't ever care about me. That was her manipulation tactic. She was worried about her secret and feeding her ego. She was also trying to take my baby from me. I don't know why. She had a difficult time caring for the one she had and her three older stepchildren. Not to mention caring for herself and where her attention is needed there. I never felt safe with her being around. She was just looking for a way to destroy me.

Darla would find out where I was working and tell her second husband, Robert, the police chief. He called using his networking. Those two were getting into everything I was accomplishing in life. Dora was doing it too. I think Darla was using Dora too. Those two supported each other there. Knowing what they were doing and not being able to do anything about it, placed a very heavy weight on my mind. They'd cause unnecessary financial hardships for me hoping I couldn't keep my baby financially. That was the first time I said "no more" to what they were doing to my life. I have my little daughter and family now to look out for as well. I think her husband Robert was trying to make a name for himself in Arizona. I heard that from somewhere and that he had eyes set on partially retiring out here. I don't exactly remember from who. This state isn't big enough to hold both of us. Not the way he was going about it with Darla. Darla was using me to help her husband make contacts in Arizona. They were trying to ride on my coattails into Arizona and they were doing it in all the wrong way. When Barry and I bought our house together, I was so happy and called Darla to tell her our good news. She said, *"Is there a place to park an RV?"* I think Robert wanted what I had too. Either one of them has a clue as to what I was accomplishing with my education and all the hard work I put into that. They both thought they could trample right over me on that. I was becoming disheartened, not knowing what to do about them. It is surprising that I could keep my head under the hardships they were throwing at me. What they were doing placed a serious emotional strain on me. That's because I knew and I could do nothing about that. That was distressing and exhausting to me and they thought it was really funny.

At one time Barry thought I was delusional thinking everyone was out to get me. I had to convince him it was not everyone, just a few that was turning that into many others. As Barry sat in one of my sessions with me, my doctor said, *"I see what Darla's doing. She's using her police connections."* I gave a sigh of relief and dropped my head. I started to cry over the mess they were making out of my life. It was so tiring too and now I wasn't a lone thinker. Someone else now knows. I never once felt that I was losing my mind on that either.

· · · · ·

My husband was providing me with the no stress, non-judgmental, safe environment I needed in order to recall the memories of the horrific night. I can't precisely say when the dissociation started wearing off. When I think back, I was taking college classes and getting through them. My evil sisters weren't around either when that started happening and I had Melissa. I think Melissa triggered it, and that coupled with my tenacity on not giving up with education brought that memory forward. I was performing tasks that I could never do before. It never hit me either. I knew I needed an expert to sort out my puzzling life and explain to me what the hell had happened on that dark night of my childhood. I finally got an appointment with a psychologist. I learned about the psychologist through another social worker. I told him I wanted to talk to someone like a "Dr. Phil type" person. It did not take me long to make the decision. I asked my Barry to come with me. His support was the fuel I needed to move along, and at every instant of our life together, that support has always been there.

The time had come to attend my first session with the doctor. I began expressing my confused emotions, and within a matter of a few minutes, I was able to speak from my heart. I told him how I had left myself and didn't return until years later. It was the first time I was told that I had dissociated. He explained to me what dissociation is and that when a person dissociates they usually come back from it immediately. My case was different. It lasted for years.

He asked in amazement, *"How did you come back?"*

I explained it to him with a demonstration. With my two arms and hands extended outward in front of me, I crossed my right arm over my left to join the two into one arm while saying, *"When the two of me merged, I became one."* I was smart enough to know that. I told him that I knew whatever this thing was about me, would be over. I just didn't know when. I did see a light at the end of the tunnel and always kept that in view. He commented on how I remained positive. I had to. I was all I had.

He helped me to see everything quite clearly. He was very impressed with how I got so far in life. He couldn't believe at first that I was a postgraduate degree holder. He wondered, enthusiastically, how I managed. I just did—I don't know if I consider myself an avid reader, however, I do read a lot and look everything up that I want to know. That's a lot, too! I'm more of a self-taught person. I do consult with an expert when the need arises. He added, *"But going to school, you're not going to get anything out of it."* He was referring to my school girl days. I explained to him, back then, all a person needed was a D to pass and graduate. He then encouraged me to get my book out there to tell my story. Hopefully, it'll help someone else.

I asked the doctor, *"If a person dissociates and never comes back, do they just die like that?"**

He nodded in the affirmative.

I thought out loud and said, *"How awful, dying not ever knowing who you are, and the potential a person can reach."* I think a couple of my older brothers might be dissociated. I'm talking about the dissociation I had—localized amnesia.

· · · · ·

I saw the doctor weekly for about six months. Gradually, my visits were cut down to twice a month, then once a month, until I never again felt the need to visit him. During the latter part of our sessions, while talking to the doctor, I mentioned that one evening during our conversations the last piece of that night came to me.

I told the doctor, *"Darla had her arm over her eyes,"* and I demonstrated by placing my right arm over my eyes.

It was then that he told me about the *"third eye."*

I said, *"Before now I couldn't see anything because I didn't have keen perception or intuition. Now I feel like I'm the eye in the sky."*

He gave a nod to a framed postcard on his office desk and asked me, *"Do you know what that is?"*

I shook my head and gently shrugged my shoulders and said no. To me, it looked like a loose white cloud in the sky with a smaller blue circle in the middle where the cloud thinned out.

He said that a client gave that to him and said, *"It is the eye of God."*

In the past, I told him about a prayer I did in 1986 where I wanted feelings. That's also when he said that music evokes a lot of feelings. I couldn't agree more with that statement. I then saw the connection with Pa singing to us and music.

I never thought I could be hypnotized. That just wasn't going to happen. He asked me if my father could sing well to which I said no. One evening, while I was in a session, the doctor hypnotized me. I was lying on his sofa and he began softly singing as I went into my subconscious. I awoke at the count of three. He hypnotized me a couple of times and it was the same. After those evenings, during one of my sessions, I remembered the last memory of that night with Darla. I was talking to the doctor when that last memory came to me. I just held onto it and didn't mention it at the time. A couple of sessions later, I revealed the last piece of that night to the doctor. That's probably what the hypnosis was for. That's where Darla had her arm over her eyes. With his index finger pointed upward, fingers and thumb loosely rounded, he drew his hand up to his face, and stopped right between his eyes.

He said, *"That was your third eye!"* I never thought then that the hypnosis with the singing is where I was the night I dissociated. I connected that hypnosis with Pa singing to us as we were lying in bed.

I had to ask him, *"I'm not dissociated anymore, am I?"*

He said, *"No! You are smart and a truthful person."*

I would have never pulled off the education I did if I was dissociated. I just want to be left alone by my family and live the peaceful life I have created for myself. It was later revealed to me that Dora is a sociopath.

My doctor was a wonderful person, and if it wasn't for him, I wouldn't have ever found myself. It took a long time, but it was worth it. He finally answered my life-long question as to who I am.

· · · · ·

One evening, I called Rosey and asked her about that night. I just opened with, *"I remembered the night when Pa did something to Darla."*

She said, *"What did you just say?"*

I repeated myself. She indeed verified that night did happen just like I said it did. I told her about my dissociation and that I was seeing a doctor, a psychologist, over what happened that night.

That's when she said, *"They always thought you weren't paying attention."* She said that as if, mystery solved. She asked me to ask the doctor to pull something else out of me because there was something else I needed to know.

I said, *"He didn't pull anything out of me. I had this all remembered before I went to go see the doctor. "Just tell me—I don't remember any more."*

I waited long enough to find the truth. I didn't want to wait anymore. I think she thought I was seeing some kind of a witch doctor that used magic cards, tea leaves, and potions. Eventually, Rosey was a big help with corroborating my memory of that night. I also called Marie and mentioned that night to her.

She said, *"Whoooo!"* in a high-pitched voice. *"You were so little. You remembered that?"*

To which I answered, *"Yes."*

I asked both of them why didn't anyone call the police? Both answers were, *"They wouldn't have done anything in those days."* I still sometimes think, *"How would they know when no one ever tried."* I still think they would have done something.

. . . . .

One day, thinking about my sessions with the psychologist, I called Darla. She answered the phone.

I said, *"I was calling because I know you."*

She angrily snapped, *"You don't know me,"* hung up and refused to carry on with the conversation.

I waited a couple of days and called her again. She answered the phone and said, with a giddy, evil chuckle, *"Yes, Graci?"* I know *she* thought I was calling about what happened at my work once her and her husband got in there with their phone calls.

My nickname has been Graci since childhood. I said, *"I'm calling to tell you that I know you."*

She replied in a shouting, angry voice, *"You don't know me!"*

I said calmly, *"Yes, I do."*

She continued to angrily shout over me. *"No, you don't!"*

"Yes, I do."

After our third round of this, she angrily shouted in a matter-of-fact voice, *"You don't know me!"*

I calmly said, *"I do, too."* I forced in, *"You're a double dealer and you use tools."*

By that, I meant other people. I was starting to give an example of a clueless person she used at one time when I noticed a long silence and didn't think she was on the phone any longer. I just quietly hung up. She heard me though. With her shouting at me, I thought that must be a tactic she learned hoping I'd submit. She was indeed quite defensive.

I then called Dora. Since Dora also referred to our father as Pa, I told her I remembered when Pa did something to Darla. However, I left the word "night" out of the statement on purpose. I wanted to hear her say it. I wanted to know she went back there.

She gleefully and lightheartedly said, *"That was a long time ago, and nobody even cares about that anymore, that was so far in Darla's past."* As if others knew. She made that night sound so trivial. If I didn't know any better, I'd think that happened to everybody.

I answered, *"I care, and I remembered you're the one that wanted to start slap-ping me."*

She fearfully said, *"I don't remember anything about that night."*

There it was. She hung up on me.

Both Dora and Darla would find what they perceived as a person's weak-nesses and expose them to their higher-ups at work, school, wherever they could make a financial impact. They did that with anyone they didn't like and I was their main target. They'd make up stories and embellish as they went along. Dora and Darla both projected a lot onto me and other people, I'm sure. Everything they didn't like about themselves, they gave to me. They'd sound self-righteous and talked a good game. The only reason their game lasted so long is because I was dissociated. They took advantage of that. Dora would call or make a visit and talk to schools, social circles, and employers. It would be anyone whose reputation she could damage.

Darla was like that too. Darla also had the best connections to do what she was doing. They were both obsessed with my life and what I was doing. What they were doing was bad and unethical. I still find it hard to believe they got away with that for as long as they did. Robert never questioned Darla's integrity. Because of his professional status, no one ever questioned him. He's supposed to know what he's doing. After trying to keep the dirty family secret, Rosey said that there was no one Dora and Darla hated more than they hated me. If she only knew what they'd say about her when she wasn't around! I'm sure I was the most hated. I don't know why. I never did anything to either one of them. I've always given them whatever I possibly could. Barry made a comment that I did a lot for them. I've also helped both of them in this lifetime when they hit an unkind rough patch. When I should have been the one that they wanted to help. I wouldn't be at all sur-prised to learn they had secret agendas against each other on taking what I brought to the table. I say that humbly. That looked pretty good to them. I did in life what they didn't want to. However, they wanted what I had. I wasn't worried either. Dora and Darla both had a fit when they learned Barry and I were getting married, according to Rosey. They were way too obsessed with my life. I think they wanted to do what I did but didn't want to do the work I did to get to where I am. So, they just thought they'd take mine because I don't pay attention. Darla could also use her husband to get at me. And that she did.

· · · · ·

I always thought Darla was content with working office clerk jobs and through employment agencies. She sews really well, too. She also is a beautician. I guess that isn't what she really wanted. Dora worked as a cashier at Kmart in my hometown. It's really sad what happened to her family. My niece Carolyn did well and is married with two grown boys and is now a grandmother herself. Martin is also married with two grown children and he is a grandfather. All of my brothers did well too. Vaughn is a machinist. James worked for the steel plant and Doug retired from Ford motor. Rosey is also retired from the gas company and a grandmother. I'm out here in the Southwest with my own family and we aren't dysfunctional. I learned all about unconditional love from Barry. What a beautiful man both inside and out. Melissa makes us both very proud. She is a scientist.

Chapter 15

On my last visit, after my doctor solved the puzzle of my life along with me, he briefly mentioned mandated reporting. I did call the police in my hometown to report the crime that I remembered when I was four years old.

I got to speak to a savvy officer that knew about trauma and dissociation. She gave me a voice and listened to what I had to say. I wanted to bow out of being my family's scapegoat and at the same time, I didn't want to leave anyone at risk. I'm not their scapegoat anymore. That type of child abuse can repeat itself and manifest itself in other ways, too. I know they can't place that on me anymore. After speaking to the officer, I felt a sense of calm and peace inside of me as if I knew everything was going to be fine. That particular officer was really smart. I spoke my heart out. At one point, I briefly felt like I was four years old again. Finally, I was given a voice and someone that cared heard me and got the other side.

· · · · ·

I tried to reconcile and get on better terms with Dora and Darla while striving to make it through the daily hurdles I've had to face since childhood. Dora has done a lot of damage to other people, too. I was her main target. I never trusted them. I began to figure out more as time went on. By 2006, what they were doing to me became quite clear to me. I wanted to do something about it but didn't know what. They were calling my employers, friends, and anyone

I knew that they could get to. With me, it could have been a simple friend so-cial circle. They didn't care. as long as they could personally tear me down.

Dora and Darla described me as a dissociated person by using the worst diction. That's because they didn't know. I don't think that would have made a difference either. They were just out to make sure I never had or knew any-thing. What I did have they wanted. I don't think they could have done what I did. For starters, you have to be true to yourself. We are who we are.

In 2003, Darla and Robert came out to visit me. They stayed in my home for two weeks. I don't know why. They were good for about the first hour complete with fake smiles. Then they appeared to be miserable the entire time. Darla constantly walked around like she was smelling something foul. During that time, I also noticed how Darla's husband always wanted to be in control. One day, as I was flipping through the TV stations and found a show I liked, he grabbed the remote right out of my hand and put on a station he liked. He just sat there with the remote in his hand. He's like that; he always has been. I was surprised at his disrespectfulness, but I maintained my peace. I knew they'd never be back. They brought their own golf clubs and would get up and go golfing. I don't know if they were meeting anyone. I know they wanted to come back in 2008, but I didn't ask them anymore. They did drop a few hints of not being able to tolerate Indiana's cold winters. Robert grumbled about the icy, windy, cold weather. My response was, *"I'm glad I don't have to live in it anymore."* They sure weren't expecting that.

That's when Darla and Robert turned up their dirty work and made a phone call to my employer. That was going to be their last smear on me. They acted as if they knew me. They talked about how I grew up impoverished, wore sawed off shoes, hardly had anything to eat, never went to school, and claimed that it was why I never knew anything. They said clearly and explicitly that I was stupid and not to be trusted with any type of work because I couldn't do it. That has been working for them throughout my life and they were enjoying it. Darla was trying to play amateur detective and that was working until the doc-tor intervened and a real officer gave me a voice to hear the other side. I didn't know everything they said about me, but there were a lot of falsehoods going on. They must have said I was a criminal at some point. For example, the last place I worked asked me to go have my fingerprint clearance card updated. I already had one that was well within the expiration date. That wasn't the first time that happened either with me having to get my fingerprint card redone. I knew who was doing that but what could I do! That one was Darla's and Robert's routine. I guess he was showing off his police skills. They use the word "cop" a lot. That word turned into a big clue as to what they were doing. That was harassment, but police can do that. They didn't know I was onto them, but I didn't know what to do. At one time, Darla and Robert were trying to get me arrested. That must have gotten boring for them because I don't do anything to get arrested. I hope nobody put any money into what they were doing. If they did, that's on Darla and Robert, not on me.

Darla and her husband even questioned my competency. They said they weren't sure how I got a master's degree because I wasn't capable of doing anything successfully. They were making fun of the education I obtained. Saying, *"She might get something out of that."* That's what bullies do, isn't it? They were laughing and making fun of me when I was out there trying to make this world a better place.

All of this was because they didn't have a clue. I was less willing to submit to them and had become a rebel in my own right. Since they didn't have anything substantial against me, they began tampering with my family and education. I am a very good social worker and a writer. I know the department manager at my work wasn't happy with Darla and what her husband was doing. He knew there was more than met the eye or in this case the ear. He liked my work. He didn't care who her husband said he was. He didn't actually say that either. He didn't have to. They couldn't have been more wrong about me. I can't believe anyone would believe them without talking to me. Everyone was just hush hush and just looked at me. I know Darla knew better than her husband. I think she learned how to keep her secret hidden by being around him. She really honed her secret there. He is, after all, a police chief. I'm giving him too much credit here. Most of the men and women in law enforcement have some training in psychology, so I'm assuming he might have some too. While Darla might have known better than him, I knew better than both of them!

Darla thought and said that her husband was naturally smart and didn't need a college education. Maybe some people can do that. It'd be really nice if they could. Although, I'd be afraid to practice any psychology calls without having the education to back me up. Experience does help, but academic expertise is equally important. Especially at a Master level. For example, when diagnosing a person, not having an educational foundation could lead to making a wrong call. The detective I spoke to "silenced the lambs," which is the title I like to call that particular circumstance. Only my sisters aren't lambs, in this case, they're more like wolves in sheep's' clothing.

The officer was an amazing person. I say *"silencing the lambs"* because I could hear what Dora, Darla, and her husband were saying without me actually hearing them say it. I could tell by what other people would say to me. I knew by what another person would say and where that thought must have come from. The wording that was used was a big clue. I've been around my family long enough to know how they speak and the words they use. I just knew and I was right. Education trumps ignorance again!

. . . . .

In 1987, Dora was out to visit me for a couple of days. She was actually going to Northern California to visit my older brothers. I don't know why she came to visit me. I was struggling to keep my head afloat, and she took the opportunity to steal a shirt from me. I only had a couple of shirts. During this stay, she met a friend of mine briefly. She left happy and smiling for California. I didn't find out about the shirt until after she left.

The following year, Dora and Rosey came out together to visit me. I left them in my apartment while I went to work. I asked them to not turn up the air conditioner because I was trying to save money. While I was at work, they went to a Denny's restaurant. Dora saw the friend of mine she met in 1987. She went over to that friend and started doing her thing about what an awful, bad, and stupid person I was. She told my friend that I had a lot of psychological problems. I was later told about that same incident by my friend. After they left, I called Dora and gave her a piece of my mind. She denied it and said that my friend was lying. Rosey told me about Dora's encounter with my friend at Denny's and said she told Dora she shouldn't be talking about me like that. That didn't stop her. She told Rosey to go wait in the car. I don't know why I ever spoke to Dora again. I had an electricity bill of $400 because my sisters had used a lot of air conditioning.

Two thousand six was the last time Dora and Darla visited me. They visited me in the home Barry and I had purchased. Their intentions were getting more obvious by the day. My friend Richard was over and said he saw Darla walking around my home looking at my things while I was at work. He said, *"She had a look on her face like you weren't supposed to have those things."* I have a beautiful antique/vintage china, paintings, and cloth collection that I acquired throughout my life. Richard told me that Darla walked into the kitchen and started to say something to Dora when she noticed he was standing right there. She immediately became quiet. My daughter developed my vintage taste and timeless beauty. My husband knows what to look for.

It wasn't hard to tell that my sisters were jealous of me. I haven't been dissociated for a long time and I have been seeing both of them for who they really are. However, at that time, I still didn't know that I had been dissociated at one time. Dora tried to come back to Arizona in 2008. I was expecting that and so I called her. I didn't want her showing up on my doorstep or making any long-term plans that involved staying at my home.

She said, *"After the holidays, I'll come out and stay with you for a while. I'll help you."* She wanted to help *herself.*

Maybe when I was nineteen she could have done that. I said, *"I don't need any help."*

She said, *"No."*

"No."

That went on for about three no's. Hers were angry and each one was louder than the prior one. I suggested that she could go live with her daughter.

She angrily snapped, *"I don't want to go live over there."*

I don't know where "there" is either. I said, *"Well, I don't need any help."*

She abruptly hung up on me. I was glad that call was over. Rosey told me, after that phone call, Dora was huffing and puffing about me and what I had and if it were up to her I wouldn't have anything. She was with Darla when she said that and Darla just followed her around and remained quiet.

Clearly, she wasn't expecting that. I was in the middle of asking her to explore her other options for a place to live and that is when she hung up on me. What she was really saying in that phone call was that she wanted to move in with me. She wanted me to take care of her and there's not much you can expect from a self-centered person. She was looking for a home for her and her adult children. My home and family would have just been an empowering station for her illness. When I mentioned this part to the doctor, I could tell he became slightly nervous but was at ease again when I told him that I had declined her offer. He was relieved that I said no to her. He ensured I did not change my mind. It was several months into seeing the doctor when I called Dora and told her I remembered everything that happened in the night I became disassociated.

· · · · ·

My oldest sister Marie lives in Florida now. She told me she would see Dora whenever she visited our hometown. Dora had my mother's piano at her home like a shrine. Marie would often find Dora wearing my mother's aprons. I didn't even know those existed anymore. Dora used my mother's pots and pans as well as her rolling pin and board. Dora would ask Marie who did the piano remind her of. Dora wanted to hear our mother play as she never heard her play once. Dora once told me that she had a tape, which all of us kids do, of my mother playing the piano. Dora said she listened to that on her way to and from work, while she was working at a local Kmart. To me, that was kind of spooky because she never listened to my mother play the piano at home. Dora had no interest in music that I know of. Suddenly she wanted to listen to that tape.

One of my older brothers once said, *"Look at Dora trying to act like Ma!"* It was a time we were all visiting my brother, Joe, in Northern California. There was some kind of family reunion going on at his home. She'd walk around the kitchen like my mother did. She tried to speak in a soft voice like mother and tried to portray herself as an angelic person. She sure wasn't. When she talked she'd refer to our mother as "my mother" as if she was the only one that had a mother. She'd also say that her adult daughter was just like Graci and how her daughter reminded her of Graci. She'd say that to other people too. Hearing that from others, I could only guess where that thought came from. I never saw it. I didn't know how or even why she'd say such a thing. I know her daughter tried to mirror me. When Dora visited me, she'd take my blouses and shirts for herself. I think she was giving those to her daughter. I would find out later after she would leave my home. I don't know why she'd want her daughter to be like me. She sure isn't.

· · · · ·

When I was out in the field as a teacher, I had an adult education teaching certificate. I was teaching English as a Second Language to students. Dora told me her daughter was teaching Spanish even though her daughter doesn't speak Spanish. I don't really know what she does at all. I know she was in no way a teacher. Dora once told me that people would tell her that her daughter is spoiled. She wanted me to say something, which I never did. I realized a long time ago that whatever Dora said to me, I had to believe the opposite in order to arrive at the truth. I told my husband about it since Dora can be scary. If I didn't know any better, I'd think that Dora wanted to recreate my mother and me. She didn't get the attention she craved from my mother. My mother had a lot of kids and couldn't give Dora the attention she wanted. My mother really spread herself thin there. I was the bottom of the totem pole with the girls in my family. I think for that reason my mother did display more attention towards me. The rest were gone, married.

Both Dora and Darla were disrespectful and had serious boundary issues in my home. Whenever I visited my hometown in the past, they wouldn't even answer their door for me. I knew better than to ask them for anything. When Dora was visiting me at our home once, she brought her daughter, Juana, and grandson with her. Juana wanted to do everything I did. She was really quiet and didn't say much. She wanted any clothes I didn't want anymore. I didn't have any clothes that I didn't wear. Besides, we never wore the same size anyway. I had an old wooden spoon in a coffee can that turned up missing. A few times while she was at my home with her daughter, she'd get up to make coffee for everyone there. If I'd get up to make it she'd jump up in front of me and decide to make it. Juana went back to Indiana before she did. After Juana left, I got up to make coffee for everyone. She jumped up in front of me because she decided to do it. She didn't want me to see that spoon was missing. After Dora left I called her to kindly ask where my items went that turned up missing. I figured she gave the spoon to her daughter. I didn't care about that either. That's beside the point. I found other items missing that her daughter wanted. For example, I used an insulated sack for my lunch. That also turned up missing. Dora thought she could give away anything of mine to her daughter. She was beginning to act as if she lived in my home and that my things were hers. She did not have any limitations at all. Darla also felt entitled to my things, too, although she wasn't as bad as Dora. Dora literally stole from me. At least Darla employed manipulation techniques to try and take something of mine.

I had a large picture of my mother hanging up in my music room. Juana expressed how she wanted that. I don't know why. My mother never knew Juana and Juana never knew my mother. Dora was after the painting to have it for her daughter. I stopped the nonsense then. After they all went back home to Indiana, I called Dora to kindly ask where my items went that turned up missing. She changed the subject and told me Juana and her son-in-law bought a house. Dora was like that. She'd change the subject when confronted. She was so obvious. She said Juana *"painted one of the rooms an orange color."* I had a room in my home painted faded yellow that I called "faded tangerine." They were starting to nauseate me already.

After the economic downturn of the housing market in the early 2000s, Dora was telling others that her daughter moved and was leasing/renting her house. She said they moved to New York for work and schools. Rosey called me during this time to tell me about it. I had to believe the opposite and suggested she had lost her home. Rosey looked that up and found what I said was true. She called Dora and told her. I felt sad for her daughter. I feel for all of her kids.

I was talking to my brother Vaughn on the phone shortly afterward. I started just talking about everyday things, nothing of importance, when he said, *"There is nothing wrong with losing a home."* Dora actually thought there was something wrong with that, not me.

I replied, *"I never said there was. There is always something wrong when a person doesn't want to face reality."*

However, he hung up on me. He slammed the phone down so hard that if it was a kitchen wall phone, that phone must have fallen off the wall. Dora's daughter wanted to be just like me. She doesn't have that much time in life to go through whatever I went through, that revealed the person I am today. I'm not so sure I would wish that on anyone.

Dora's husband died in 2000. The insurance funds she received from him disappeared quickly. I think the insurance money did not last longer than a year. She sold their home and moved into a condominium. She lived there less than a year and wanted to sue the Homeowners Association for mold. She sold that place and moved into an apartment. She lived there for about a year and remarried a man from the same hometown. I kind of knew who he was, but I didn't really know him well. She moved in with him at his home. Whenever she'd see Rosey she'd ask, *"Where did all my money go?"* I kind of feel sorry for the old girl.

She wanted to move into my home for an indefinite period of time before she remarried. I don't think she wanted to marry the second time. She wanted to find a home for her and her adult children. That's a sad story in and of itself. I don't even want to think about that. She is very charismatic and charming. She was able to charm anyone and was really good at it. I still don't know how she had a meaningful conversation with anyone. Just about everything she said was a lie. She boasted about her children making accomplishments that they never made. She'd talk about what an impoverished stupid person I was to others. She'd grab her Catholic bible and run behind people quoting scriptures. Scripture applied only to others and never to herself.

She portrayed a perfect life. I know she was hiding a lot that went on in her own home. I know there are secrets there. I know there was a lot of domestic violence that went on in her home. That was directed towards her and her children by her husband. I don't know how much of anything she said to others could be believed though. Smart people knew there was something wrong with her. Her second marriage didn't last long either. Once the secret was out and I pulled her mask off, she didn't have a place to run or hide in. She had fooled many people about her perfect persona.

Dora began to behave really weird. The secret was out, and others knew who she really was. I think her second husband's family didn't want her there in his home anymore. I think his son is also a policeman. She went to go live with one of her sons for a while. She was escaping his home by climbing out of a bedroom window. Her son and his wife would have to go get her from a neighbor's home. She would tell the neighbor that her son and his wife were trying to kidnap her. She really lost it when her mask came off and the true villain was revealed. I didn't mean for that to happen to her. It just did. Rosey commented to me that, *"Dora's web of lies finally caught up to her."* She told me she visited Dora at a state hospital. Dora was in a lockdown unit. There are two staff people assigned to a patient when they take a resident outside for an hour every day. They'd allow the resident to walk around in a fenced area that wasn't very big. There were no mirrors in her room. Rosey thought that was odd. I had nothing to say. Both Dora and Darla had an obsession with me. They wanted to keep me silenced forever about the secret.

Chapter 16

Darla and Dora are more or less the same. Darla's not as charming as Dora is, though, not that I've experienced being around her. She always looked like she was looking for evil ways to satisfy her ego. I don't think I've ever seen her smile. Unless she was doing something underhanded and mean to me. Hurting me really made her happy. She'd actually laugh at the dirty deeds she was doing to me. Both her and her husband laughed. They really enjoyed entertaining themselves by tearing me down. I do know that Darla didn't want certain people talking to me or me talking to them. If she couldn't get a person to stop talking to me, she'd say something derogatory to me about that person, hoping I'd not talk to that person anymore. These were usually people who, if they knew our family secret, would have access to someone that knew her husband in his line of work.

Darla had a disdain for strong independent women too. The last time Darla was out visiting me, I was watching a show on TV. She said, *"Only stupid people watch shows like that."* I think the show was *Inside Edition*. She's not a pleasant person to be around. She was always telling me that I couldn't ever succeed with anything in life. She always sees the worst of anything and goes by that. She lives her life by that. Her favorite object is a mirror. Growing up she'd stay up in her room and look into her makeup mirror. That seemed like an all-day thing for her. She practices smiling and facial expressions in the mirror. She is a perfectionist.

I lived in Washington state for a year, but I wanted to come back to Arizona. I felt so alone in Washington. I was working for the Department of

Health Services. I called and spoke to Darla. I just wanted to hear a familiar voice for support. I had met an unstable lady that told me she set fire to her car. Of course, I reported that. What a mistake that was to call Darla. Both she and her husband began calling the police in the town I was in. They were doing their networking thing. God only knows what they gained wanting me to be falsely known as a bad person.

While I was there, they told my acquaintances from work that I was Mexican and that I pretended I wasn't. They were making me sound like I was an arrogant person without an education. A reliable source from my hometown told me that Darla actually does that. I wasn't surprised. I was laid off from there. Even though I sensed something was wrong, I didn't think they'd actually do something like that to me. I could tell by the words of a co-worker as he was once speaking to me. Those were not his words, but Darla's. They wanted to render me weak, helpless, and financially dependent on them. Not that they'd help either. They sought pleasure in hearing me beg. I never did though. I knew better. They were really good at what they were doing and almost succeeded in silencing me forever.

When I called Darla one last time from Washington, she said excitedly, *"Oh, I'll come out there and get what you've got."* Instead of sympathizing, she wanted everything that I had.

She added, *"Robert said he wouldn't mind going there."* They were looking for a free vacation to Washington, hopefully paid for by the city. Robert is from a really small town and was trying to get noticed anywhere and without doing anything notable either. Nothing to be noted for anyway. Darla was trying to help him with that too by using me. In my opinion, if he wanted that kind of notoriety, a larger inner-city is where to start and gain experience. He'd have had better exposure to a much more diverse population. It would be a bad idea to go from a Maybury town to a larger metropolitan inner-city like I live in. That's just my opinion.

With that phone call, Darla made that sound like I was going somewhere. My heart dropped and you could hear that sadness in my voice. How dare she? I didn't have that much and just the thought of her coming and taking what I had was unbearable. Who did she think she was? What right did she have? They were just trying to get a free trip to Washington. He was doing his networking thing wanting to show off his cop skills and she wanted others to see how beautiful and perfect she was. I didn't talk to her anymore while I was there. I came back to Arizona right after that. I figured they were doing something. They didn't know I knew they were up to something. I wasn't quite sure what. I actually didn't find out until a couple of years later. That's however, when I became very leery of what was going on with them and it wasn't good. Not for me anyway.

Darla would make lies or stories to have a person not talk to me or vice versa. This one time she told me that my cousin, who I have a relationship with, said to her oldest stepdaughter, Karen, *"Graci's mother had fourteen children and all from different men."* Karen and my cousin work together. Those thoughts can only come from a very sick person. I know he never said that.

I have to laugh at Dora and Darla sometimes. Some of the weird things they say are funny. Darla does not allow for anyone else to have an opinion. Her way is the only way. She angers quickly when another opinion is voiced about anything. She can sound really mean to that person. Once, Robert was kind of laughing at her because her son moved out of state. He said, *"She's going through the mom withdrawals."* Darla angrily snapped back, *"None of your kids ever left you."* I actually couldn't believe she said that using that tone. Not one hair can be out of place and she's very vain if it does fall out of place. Don't dare tell her if it is. I'm so glad I don't have them around anymore. They never wanted to see me have anything. What I did have, they wanted, no matter how little it was. That included the men in my life too.

Part 4

All's Well that Ends Well

Chapter 17

During my later sessions with the psychologist, I learned that what happened that night to my sister, also had happened to our father. I mentioned to my doctor that the only thing I know about my father is that he grew up in an orphanage in Mexico. Thinking out loud he said, *"An orphanage in Mexico."* I didn't know the name of it or if it even still existed. Like many other forms of repetitive abuse, that night was no different. I couldn't have known much about it if it wasn't for my therapy sessions with the psychologist. When I told him what Rosey verified for me, he said, *"I don't know if what you saw is all that caused you to dissociate. I only know about the one you're telling me."* He was talking about the only one I remembered. I don't know if that was all that went on or how many times it happened to Darla. Rosey verified more that I didn't remember. Is it possible that I witnessed other traumatic events that I don't remember because I was still so very young myself,? Yes, it is very possible. It could have happened to other siblings and on other days. I just don't remember. The psychologist reassured me that I wasn't dissociated anymore. I remembered the one incident I needed to. The one that caused me to dissociate and lose touch with reality.

I was thinking out loud in a session and said, *"I wonder who she blamed the other times."*

The doctor said, *"Darla was the primary victim and you were a secondary victim because you were the scapegoat. It's much easier to beat up on a four year old child."*

I briefly mentioned this to another doctor at another time, unrelated to my trauma. She added, *"They could control a four year old child."* That was still going on today. My doctor said more than once during my sessions, *"What a dysfunctional family!"* He said that with conviction.

He also asked me, *"Why do you think they blamed you and never told on him?"*

To which I answered, *"Because of who it was."*

He added, *"He put the fear in them."*

I asked, *"On a scale of one to ten, with ten being the highest, where does my family dysfunction fall?"*

He said, *"Yours is right up there."*

I took that as a ten. I also asked him where I fell on the dissociation scale, to which he answered, *"You were right up there."* Again, I took that as a ten. When I told the doctor. this was a second marriage for both Darla and Robert, he asked with concern, *"Are there children?"*

. . . . .

After my final session I decided to call my hometown's police. I left a message for an officer to return my call. The message was not complex. It was all about the repressed memory surfacing that reminded me of the crime that was committed.

It had been a couple of days since I left the message. I never thought I'd hear back. Who in law enforcement wanted to hear from me or believe me? I never thought I'd be heard. I was in the back room of my house working on the computer, listening to some music, when my phone rang. It was an officer returning my call. I was very happy to hear from her. I knew it was my only chance and I had to make it count. I turned the music off and started talking. I didn't even want to breathe or stop for periods. I feel I was lucky that I coincidentally reached an officer who was savvy to trauma and dissociation. From talking to her I knew that she was well aware of this subject. The officer really listened to what I had to say. Even though I knew the secret was a very old one, to me it still mattered and needed to be told. Sometimes the truth takes a long time. The secret had spread significantly, and it was a secret that should have never been kept hidden. In some places it might even be illegal to keep secrets of child abuse and never talk about them. We all know what it did to me.

. . . . .

Just before I spoke to the hometown police, I knew what Dora, Darla, and her husband were up to. They wanted to keep me silenced about the secret. Darla's husband didn't even know the secret. That's how well they had hidden the information. That was their motive in helping Darla's husband with his networking to wherever I was working and with whom I socialized. With a master's degree, social circles can become really thinned out with just a few members. However, those social circles are the best ones I ever formed. I was told earlier on that Robert was trying to make a name for himself where I live. Maybe he has grandkids he needs to employ. Who knows. He brags about scoring so very high on the civil service test. That means nothing. That test they take just means a person can take a test and pass it. All you need is a 70% to pass that test. It doesn't matter if you score a 70 or a 95 either. It just means you can pass a test. I don't see where that tests critical thinking skills. He missed all of the classic projection that was being thrown at him. That's what Darla and Dora were doing. Projecting what they didn't like about themselves onto me. I wouldn't brag about that if it were me. An education is much more important and critical. "The whole purpose of education is to turn mirrors into windows." (Sydney J. Harris) They do know laws and other things people don't know. I wondered where is that projection coming from with me being a stupid criminal. The officer I spoke to knew. That officer is not from Maybury. She was connecting dots with amazing accuracy. This is just my thought, maybe someone they know was arrested for drugs and they brushed that under the rug. Never to be heard of again. Hush! Hush! There was a big write up in a local city's newspaper where there was a drug bust. All others were sent away during that time, locked up. Maybe the person they know didn't have to answer for that. Again, hush! Hush! I don't know how much truth there is to this, but his daughter told me once that she didn't have a high school reunion because she flunked out of the 12th grade. I'm using the word flunked because she had no excuse. She had a home with one or both parents. I'm sure he got her employed somewhere.

The reason Darla and Robert never had any kids between themselves is because she had herself fixed to where she can't have anymore. I think that was a pre-marital agreement. He wanted no more kids he had to be legally responsible for. So Darla put her whole life on hold to live for him and his family.

Their wish was her command. I never told her to put her life on hold to live for someone else. I heard a rumor once where his father fathered a love child he had to pay support to. Maybe that traumatized Robert. They were calling CPS on me to try to take Melissa from me. They would have taken her over mine and Barry's dead body. What a self-centered narcissistic family that is. I want to say the narcissist farm but I won't. Another thing I'll keep to myself. I felt sorry for her son. I understood his kids were mean to him. Darla just stood by and allowed that to happen.

For Robert's work, they didn't even have full time employees. His friend, father, and I think daughter all worked there part time. Robert just babysat a phone and maybe sometimes directed traffic. That's all he's ever done. A larger town would have been his answer to police work, if that's what he wanted. You can't arbitrarily make a criminal.

I was really onto them since the early '90s. I just didn't let them know. During the gaps of not seeing them, I'd actually forget about what they were doing to me. When I'd see them when they came out to visit, weird things started happening to me again and that reminded me to be cautious. I didn't know what to do about that because of the connections Darla was using. Calling my hometown police several times and lacking the confidence to say anything, I'd just hang up without leaving any real message. I felt as though I was hitting three dead ends and a stop sign. I was afraid they wouldn't listen, and I'd be wasting my time and making myself look foolish. I also had to say what our father was all about. I'd have to mention the severe dysfunction of my family too. Those were the hardest parts. The non-caring family I had is one of the reasons I wouldn't say anything about my family to anyone. Now I had to talk about it.

Not only that, but I would have to tell them I had been dissociated. I wanted someone really smart to talk to because I knew what they were saying about me to keep their secret concealed. I just never knew what to do about that. My doctor gave me the confidence, knowledge, and support I needed to make that phone call and follow through with it. This was my window of opportunity and I took my chances.

When I talked to the doctor in the beginning of my sessions, I started out saying how I had left once and came back a long time later. He asked me how

I came back. I said I just snapped out of it. He asked how I snapped out of it. I started to tell him about that night. When evil Dora was coming at me with her open raised hand. He said, with a very caring sadness in his eyes and voice, *"What did they want you to do?"* After a brief pause, he explained that was when I split, and that memory went into an inaccessible part of my consciousness causing me to dissociate. He gave me the words to explain what happened to me that night. I mentioned to him that I knew something happened, referring to the dissociation. I just didn't know what exactly that was. I told him I knew that one day that would be over. I just didn't know when, or how long it would take. I kept positive about that too. I had to get away from members of my family that brought stress and anxiety to me every day. I came from a very dysfunctional family. They are stressful to be around and too much for me. Because of their toxicity, that memory lay dormant and fortunately, years later, it did surface and freed me. The doctor explained all about dissociation to me. When I told him I didn't remember the fourth grade at all, he said, *"That's like amnesia."* With that phone call I made to my hometown police, the scapegoat came in from the wilderness. I sensed a calmness and knew at the moment I took my power back from my sisters. The scapegoat gave back every part of life she carried around that belonged to the others. She gave them what they owned. Lifted it right off the scapegoat's shoulder.

When I first talked to the hometown police, I mean really talked to them, I was a bit weary at first. I thought I was being judged at the beginning of that phone call. After a sentence or two, I knew then the officer had given me a voice. It must have been something the officer said that made me feel at ease. I knew I was being listened to and I was heard. I spilled my heart out. For a very brief time, I felt like I was four years old again. I actually re-lived that traumatic night. Revealing the secret that unmasked the true antagonists sure felt so good.

I knew I didn't want to be their scapegoat anymore. At that time, I also didn't want to leave anyone at risk. It mattered because the two sisters were still scapegoating me for that incident and were not dealing with the real issue at hand. I'm sure jealousy played into the scapegoating. For me, the more powerful motivator was the secret. I know for sure that Darla hadn't dealt with what happened to her that night, not in a healthy way. Not even her husband knew about the incident that transpired. The officer must have sensed I was frightened to talk to them and informed me that I'd be protected. I told everything I knew about that night. I never really thought of this, but I was a four-year-old eyewitness. My conscience did not allow me to hang up without telling the officer that Darla's husband did not know anything about her dark side. The officer actually said something along the same lines the doctor did about abuse and how it repeats itself. That's what made me think about Darla's dark side and how her husband didn't know. All I wanted was my sisters to leave me and my family alone. At the same time, I didn't want to leave anyone at risk either. Letting out the secret was a relief. It was an amazing feeling to not have to worry about them anymore. When I told the doctor about the snide remarks Darla and her husband were saying about me obtaining my master's degree, he said in an as a matter of fact voice, *"You raised the bar on the master's degree."*

What a wonderful doctor! He lifted me up when they put me down. I also admire Maya Angelou when she says, *"I shall rise."* I also realized I was doing nothing wrong in revealing the secret of child abuse. That needs to be brought to light and awareness must be made in order to prevent further occurrences. Secrets of that magnitude will hinder a person, repeat themselves, and destroy a family. Hopefully, by me going through dissociation, that too can be recognized and dealt with much sooner. I realized that it's never too late to tell the truth!

· · · · ·

A few months after the secret was out, I felt liberated from the constant emotional torture caused by my sisters. That weighed heavy on my mind. With thoughts of that did me no favors throughout my life. Their happy fun time was finally over. They were no longer able to make my life miserable. I felt at peace with myself too. I can rest assured they'll leave my daughter alone. Since then, there is no more talk from anyone based on the rumors of Dora, Darla, and her husband. It has all been silenced, which has allowed me to sense calmness. I can go and be whoever I want to be now.

· · · · ·

I once received an angry, name-calling Facebook text from Dora's eldest son. It wasn't worth a response. I noticed that his Facebook page was taken down the next day. I never heard any more from him.

My older sister Rosey, who still lives in my hometown, called me. She was angered by my act of calling and talking to the police. Angry and mean, she told me that Darla's husband bought her a brand-new Cadillac SUV. The tone in her voice was saying, *"Darla has a brand new toy, what do you have?"* It's always about material possessions with Darla. Rosey added, *"Darla said they just bought a ranch home and Robert paid cash for it."* I thought, *he probably has the cash as he, nor she, spends on anything else and mooch off of others as much as they can.* She also said, *"That happened to other families back then, too."*

I replied, *"That doesn't make it right. None of what you're telling me makes it right."*

There is nothing trivial about what happened that night. That is a very serious offense against a child and it needed to be brought to light and dealt with by the proper authorities. No matter how old the child abuse is. That secret destroyed my family and ruined a big portion of my life. That needed to be dealt with a long time ago. I had dreams unfulfilled and I'm not settling for anything less. Other lives in my family were destroyed as well. That also explained so much. Rosey is one of the four elder sisters who was also there that night and was able to corroborate my memory. For helping me with that, I give her respect. She may not see it now, but she will in time. I told her that I did what I had to do and that I'm a mandated reporter. We just hung up, obviously, not in a very pleasant manner.

She called me a few times after that. She wanted me to know that Dora was in a state hospital. I know she's in a lockdown unit. The patients go out for an hour, then back to the lockdown unit. No one goes to visit her. Rosey felt sad for Dora's situation. She said that Darla said she doesn't think about that night anymore and doesn't care about something that happened 100 years ago. *"I care, and that didn't happen 100 years ago."* I will not dismiss that as trivial as Darla and

Dora make it sound. In fact, it's still going on today. Not for me though. I have since allowed closure to take it from here. What they do is between them and God. Rosey was reluctant to speak to me anymore about anything that has a family member involved in any way. I think she's afraid because I went to the police once. It saddens my heart to see my family so divided as ours is.

· · · · ·

The doctor explained to me that emotions are a very big part of dissociation. He explained to me about it after I told him about me praying one night to have feelings. Similar to *The Wizard of Oz*'s Dorothy, Scarecrow, Cowardly Lion, and Tinman, I asked for feelings. I had forgotten what it was like to have them. Afterward, I had a heart to heart with God. Today, God and I are real good. The prognosis is good for a sufferer of localized amnesia dissociation if the person can remember the trauma. In helping them to remember, a safe, no stress, nonjudgmental, and supportive environment is required. Bottom line, they need to be taken out of a toxic environment where they can thrive.

Chapter 18

The amnesia dissociation that I had lasted for over three decades. It is a very awful state to be in. Sometimes when I go back in time, it's hard to believe that no one was able to identify it. It's even harder to believe that I survived and came out with no addictions. I used to tell others that I was the most likely candidate to be a drug addict. I had a couple of close calls growing up all alone in this world with people following me around. The only good part of being dissociated is that anything a person would do and say to me, that was meant to hurt and bring me down, never had a lasting impact. It didn't even register with me. The dissociation kept me protected there. It unleashed itself being married to Barry. I feel like I was actually raised with Barry and not my family. All of their unkind words and bullying tactics just rolled off my back. A friend I met while working for the steel company noticed that, when someone said something unkind to me, I would just ignore it. She thought that was amazing. By the grace of God, I got this far in life and I'm still not done yet. Would I do this all over if given the chance? Surely not—I'd pass.

During my sessions, when I asked if a person never really self-actualizes to discover who they truly are and if they die like that, I thought, what a horrible way to die. Not ever knowing who we truly are, let alone being able to write our own script.

. . . . .

I used to wonder how Dora is going to survive in the hospital. I was told that no one goes to visit her. She has no phone and cannot make anyone's life miserable by staying in there. That was something she was so used to doing. It was what she lived for and thrived on. She called every one of my employers and got to anyone that knew me. She can't do any of that to me anymore or to anyone for that matter. I was given the information that she has grown old and has been overeating. She doesn't know when to stop. The staff have to actually take the food away from her. I sure didn't mean for any of that to happen. I don't think of her anymore. With Darla, she is still married, living with her family. They'll take care of her. It has been several years since I heard from them. I don't expect to, nor want to, either. I'd just feel sorry for them.

The word that reached me was that no one from my family is allowed to speak to me anymore. The family I was born to and raised with! Maybe they never considered me as a family member. I think they're afraid I'll go to the police again. The only way I'd do that is if they are doing something wrong. Just like anyone else. I'd also expect the same from others as well. So, they don't have to worry about that anymore. I still don't want to hear from them, though. It was hard for me but I do forgive them for what they've done to me. The doctor asked me to. That doesn't mean that it was okay, free pass, or that we'll ever be running buddies. It just means that I've reached a state of closure and have moved on with my life. None of the family members ever talked to me unless they wanted something I had, so it was somewhat expected. Them not talking to me is nothing new. It's just a continuance of their previous behavior. So no, I don't miss any of them. I don't even feel like I was raised with them. Nothing has changed there on either their end or mine. I don't think they were ever aware of this either. I certainly was. And still am.

Dora—being a sociopath—thrived in making other people's lives miserable in the cruelest way. It's what she lived for! That's how she'd hurt a person. Mostly by placing an undeserved financial strain on them. She can't do that anymore, not from where she is. That's a good thing to those of us still out here. I know being impoverished in life was something she despised. She projected all of her impoverished life onto me. She acted like she wasn't, and that made her special. She told people that I actually wore shoes that were cut off at the toes to allow my feet to fit in because my parents couldn't afford any. It wasn't me, but later I learned it was her when she was about five or six-years-old. If I was impoverished growing up, what does that make them? She has never been a good thinker. I think both she and Darla lack insight. I think that might be because they are a fractured child trapped in an adult body. I wasn't even born during the post-Great Depression years. I didn't come around until the '50s. And no, I never wore sawed off shoes.

. . . . .

During my final sessions with the doctor, I was thinking out loud about why Pa never physically did anything to me. That's because he was afraid of me. He knew that I knew the secret. What that man was about did get to me in another way. That old man really went out of his way to be nice to me throughout the years.

Darla or anyone else that was present there that night didn't know about dissociation. I think they just thought that I was scared to discuss what happened that night. I'm not sure if they knew I remembered. Or Darla was hoping I really didn't see anything and didn't know. By the way, Darla would test me throughout the years regarding certain childhood memories that occurred around that time. She probably thought the memory of that night had left me with the following sunrise.

This is something I want people to know. When dissociation takes place within a person, a person is reported to look at themselves during any traumatic experience as if they are not themselves, but a different person observing themselves. There is a book titled *The Stranger in the Mirror* that describes this process. It wasn't the case with me. I didn't see anything throughout my life. Not as an observer anyway. Well, only once. That's when I actually dissociated and didn't come back to myself.

When I look back in retrospect, I now see myself as if I'm looking at a person that was never present. Just someone walking around and going places as if it wasn't my own life, but a movie I was watching. I had become a person who had no identity. I didn't know who I was or what I wanted to be. When I was actually dissociated, I just moved around in places alone. That's an awful state to be in and I had a family that didn't care. To me, that was embarrassing in and of itself. I never knew what to say about them. The only concern they had was to keep their secret a secret. All of it at the expense of my wellbeing. I paid the ultimate price and they didn't care. It sure was worth every bit of work I put into obtaining my education too! That was a very difficult task. I've always been one to constantly look everything up. That's how I learn. I'm still like that today. Google is awesome! Daily, I'm learning something new. There's a lot to know in this world.

Chapter 19

After having my memory corroborated, I also learned that there were good times with my siblings. However, not many. They sure didn't like me at all. The problem was mostly my older sisters and Vaughn. All of it felt as if a huge part of my memory was retrieved. Darla and my older brother experienced a lot together. I'd think how nicely they got along even though neither one of them spoke very much. None of the other ones got along that well, not unless they were talking down about a person. Sometimes my intuition would sweep over and nudge me when I was together with Darla and Vaughn. Sometimes it just felt awkward. I could never think of or see anything though. Still, my intuition would nudge at me, but I would be least bothered. Maybe it was because of the seating arrangement they had when Darla's second husband was present. I could never find anything though.

When Darla married the second time, she married way above herself. She was "moldable" though. It's probably a good thing her first marriage didn't work. Jerry was a serious drug addict. I liked him though and we did get along. I just don't think he wanted to be married and didn't want anyone going behind him cleaning up after himself. The second time she married when afros, shag cuts, or long straight hair parted in the middle were trending. Orange, avocado green, or harvest gold were popular colors back then. Many homes had shag carpeting. Shag carpeting with any one of those colors. I lived in an underground apartment. A person had to walk in and down a few steps to get to my door. The colors in that apartment were orange with shag carpeting and a brown with orange motif colored indoor and outdoor carpeting in the kitchen. All appliances were harvest gold. I lived there for five years. It was my last apartment in Indiana.

I never saw Darla or her husband together before they got married. I went to their wedding with my friend Ann. I wore a black crepe dress with some red print. It came below the knee and slit on one side. The dress pulled up and tied over one shoulder. I had waist length silky shiny black hair. When I walked in, I noticed the unpleasant look on Darla's face when she looked over at me. Her big eyes looked right at me and her facial expression was flat and mean as she turned her head to see who walked in. She didn't smile and looked unhappy to see me. Her face was expressionless. If looks could kill, I wouldn't be writing my story. However, I was there. I felt awkward and thought maybe I shouldn't have come. I sat down quietly next to Ann. That was a nice wedding. We all had fun. Darla's friend was the maid of honor and her brother was the bartender. I didn't know anyone at the wedding party. No one in my family ever talked to me about anything. They'd have family gatherings and cookouts and I knew nothing about them until they were over. Someone would tell me much later.

I walked over to the bar to get a drink. The bartender looked right at me and said, "Wow—who are you?"

I said, Darla's younger sister!"

He said, *"She never even told me she had a sister, and I thought Darla was the pick of the litter."*

How funny. Darla had known these people for years. I wasn't surprised. I just let that roll off and asked for a soda. I told her that I was happy for her while leaving. I don't remember going home from there. That's the first time that I saw the man she married. I never officially met him that I can remember. I kind of could tell, back then, that he had a wandering eye.

Ever since I was growing up, I heard a lot about how pretty Darla was and that she was the prettiest girl in our hometown. Those comments were promoted by Dora and the other sisters together. I thought there were a lot of pretty girls in that town and she wasn't the prettiest. I kept that to myself. Dora would say that Darla's husband saw her and thought she was beautiful and wanted to marry her. Maybe that was the case; I don't know. That's what Dora said so it might or might not be true. My family members talked about how pretty and beautiful Darla was every time they saw me. I didn't know why they did that. I'd just let them talk. They seemed to be enjoying it.

Once Darla told me how her husband thought about how he and she were the only two sane people in my family. I thought finally, at least something different. I let that roll off my back, too. When something rolled off my back, I just wouldn't say anything. Darla would always make a point of telling me someone's opinion of her and how she was better than me. She was always making a point of how pretty others thought she was. I never cared about that. I just had no comment. There has to be more to a person than just that. I kind of knew she and the others were trying to make me have a low opinion of myself in any way possible. I never did though since I never had any opinions.

On one of my last visits, I was getting ready to come back to Arizona. I went to Darla's house for some reason that I still don't remember. She, Karen, and Robert came outside to meet me in the driveway. Darla had her hair in braids wrapped around her head looking like Tia Tiola. She liked adopting *"The Little House on The Prairie"* look. She stood to my right. Her tall, thin stepdaughter, Karen, stood in front of me. Karen said to me, *"Darla is the black-haired bombshell. My mother plays the piano."* She meant her biological mother. The way she said that was as if her voice wasn't connected to her brain. Her head was wobbly too. She reminded me of a toy where you tap on the head and it springs back and bounces. That's Karen! Darla was just staring at me waiting for a response. The look Darla gave me was just short of batting her eyes. She remained extremely quiet, as always. Her husband, standing off to my left, had short permed grayish black hair. He looked off straight ahead into the breezy warm air with a smirk on his face. I didn't give a response. Apparently, Darla would manipulate others to say brainless things to me. Being dissociated, I didn't care what anyone said or thought. I just wanted someone to tell me who I was. I think my *"I don't give a damn"* attitude got to them. Not in a nice way either. Like the man at the hospital that reported I fell asleep.

The following morning, I left. I paid my last visit there. I really didn't have to see them anymore. In the past, whenever they came to visit, they always made a mess. Dora left phone cards folded in half on the bedroom floor. They'd leave clothes behind, too. I'd think that maybe Dora needed room in her suitcase. Darla and Dora would find out who, what, where, when, and how about my inner circles while in that room. I used that for my home office at that time. Darla would go home and inform her husband of her latest findings about me. The findings happened to be my most recent achievements. Yes, they invaded my privacy and it was really dirty what they were doing. Dora did as much damage to my personal and professional life as she could. They both did that. It was the main purpose of their visits. They had to keep boosting their egos. They really thought I wasn't smart at all. They continued to think I wasn't paying attention either. That sure turned around and bit them in the ass!

Years later I went back one last time to Carolyn's son's wedding. That just reminded me of how much I don't miss my family back there or that place. That was in 2008. I only was there for two days and I stayed with Carolyn. Nobody came over to visit with me. They knew I was there too. I rented a car and took myself around if I wanted to go somewhere as Carolyn was working. At the reception hall, I sat alone at a table. I saw Darla, Robert, Dora, and a friend of Dora's, her soon to be second husband, who were approaching my table. I thought, *"How nice, they're going to sit with me after all."*

Dora said, *"We just stopped by to say hi."*

Her friend sat down at my table. Darla and Robert just stood there and stared. Robert actually gave me a kiss on the side of my head. What a phony! What was that! The kiss of death! Darla just glared.

Then they all walked over to another table far away from mine. Her friend got up and went too. He did not look happy that Dora did that. When she and her friend were leaving, she walked up to me and said, *"Stop over tomorrow."* I didn't want to hear her asking to come to my home. I told her my flight left early in the morning. It actually left a day later. She started walking out the door and stopped, turned around, stomping coming toward me with her head down, like she was mad. As she reached me, she stopped short. She lifted her head up, looked at me, and saw her friend standing next to me just looking at her. She turned back around and walked out the door. I know she knew my flight wasn't leaving for another day. I thought she wanted to say something mean to me about that.

The following day Darla came over to Carolyn's. I was still there so they did know. She just sat there quietly looking at me and didn't say a word. I didn't either. I just said, *"I'm going to sleep. My flight leaves at 7:00AM."* I went to bed, left the next morning, and I won't be going back there ever again. That was it! I thought, I see how you guys are—you don't know me when your cop friends are around. There were a few from my hometown at that wedding reception, but when they're gone, you know me again. Darla just wanted to be invited back to Arizona. Both she and Robert did. Dora, too. I never offered. That was a big clue that I'm not dissociated anymore.

I saw my brother James at the reception. He was with his wife. He married a beautiful Italian girl the second time. She came over and was talking to me. She told me that she and James went to the Vietnam wall with another couple friend of theirs and James was looking all over the wall at names. He came across the names of the guys that were in the foxhole with him in 1965, he started gently running his fingers over their names when he started crying out loud and hard. She wanted to stop him but his friend said, *"No, don't stop him."* God bless his heart, all of them. James is 71 now. *Many years have passed since he was 13 jumping on the beds.*

Chapter 20

When cell phones came out, that was like handing Dora a loaded gun. No one ever said anything to me either about what they were doing. Including anyone I worked with or for. That's because Robert and Darla wanted to keep their dirty work all hush hush. It was when a co-worker would say something to me or suddenly have a different approach to me, is when I picked up on the words and energy. It wasn't hard to sense something fishy was going on. I would then know that Darla, Robert, and Dora were making their mess. Like a black widow weaving a messy web. That was really bad what they were doing and I hope no one ever has to go through a smear like I did. Especially with Robert tearing down my education. I put a lot of hard work and hours into that. Something they wouldn't understand. They were coming along tearing that down all the while laughing and smiling. I was working for the Welfare Department and had a feeling the three of them were causing some long-distance trouble. He was using his networking on me. I was not too thrilled with his performance nor was I impressed. What could I do? She was married to him and used that to her advantage to get at me. I knew she wanted me to get arrested. I didn't do anything that would get me arrested, which is why they never succeeded. Nor was I concerned about that.

I already had my master's degree the last time they were out to visit me but didn't talk about that to them. Actually, there was no need to. I knew better by then. They would have never appreciated that. Darla went through my home office. That room was set up with an extra bed in it for company. I had my plaque on the wall. My robe and collar were to the left hanging in an open closet in full view. I didn't do that on purpose either. I was usually at work when they'd go through my rooms, closets, and drawers. Including and not limited to my bedroom and Melissa's. Yes, that was awful, and what they did was really dirty. They invaded my personal life and property. I think Darla was playing detective. I wasn't dissociated anymore and was seeing them for who they really are. I still didn't realize I came and left the state of dissociation. I just knew things were very different. They just didn't get me. If I had known better, I would've had some fun with that. I was hiding right before their very eyes in broad daylight. It is fun not being dissociated anymore. Looking back, I am reassured when I realize that I gave them sufficient clues about me not being dissociated anymore. They still thought I wasn't paying attention. Things were very different for me at that time.

I would try correcting Dora when she told one of her many long tall tales about how great she was. That was something I never did before. She was talking about how she can make pizza just like my mother.

I said, *"No you don't. Her crust was very thick. Yours is paper thin like a wafer or piece of paper."*

She said, *"That's because of my husband."* That's Dora always blaming someone else and never taking responsibility.

She also said, *"I really like your veggie cleaner."*

I told her, *"They sell those at Safeway and they're inexpensive."*

She said, *"But I like yours."*

That conversation went on for a few minutes and was going nowhere. She really wanted mine. The dissociated me would have just happily given it to her. I finally said, *"My sister-in-law gave that to me, and I want it."* She just looked at me lost for words. When Darla would point to a painting on the wall or a vintage item of mine and tell me she liked it, I stopped saying, *"Here—you can have that."*

Not knowing how dirty she was doing me and how much she hated and despised me, I'd end up giving to her whatever she said she liked of mine. She was admiring and lusting over my antique china collection. She looked in my china cabinet and said, *"I'm going to an antique store to buy some chipped teacups so I can have a tea party with my grandkids."*

She was hoping I'd say, *"Oh, you poor retired thing, living on a limited income! You don't have to do that! Here—take some of mine."* That's what the dissociated me would have done.

She tried that one twice on me. It didn't work though. After my husband learned how much damage they were doing to my wellbeing and didn't care about me, he said, *"You did everything for them. Always giving them your things."* He thought I did a lot for them and couldn't believe what they were doing to me all the time. They were so hateful to me. After a while, he sure didn't like them at all. He doesn't want them out visiting anymore. We agree on that one.

· · · · ·

The day before Darla left my home was the last time she was out to visit. She said, referring to my master's degree, *"Robert said she might get something out of that."* That sure was a put down. As if he was the smartest person ever and knew what was best for me or anyone else. She was still thinking I wasn't smart and not paying attention. They did a lot of mean evil acts like that to me whenever they visited. I sure did get more than something out of my master's degree. That brought out the very best of me. When I said this to my doctor is when he said in a firm as a matter of fact voice, *"You raised the bar on the master's degree."*

Some of the last words Darla said to me the last time she and Dora were out were, *"Do you think we're jealous of you?"* I didn't reply. It wasn't worth a response. I probably would have been right to say, *"Hell yes!"* My doctor did when I told him. I just didn't want to start anything. I just wanted them to be gone. They were always ungrateful, unhappy, rude, crude, and socially unkind when they came to visit me. I never cared about looks and I still don't. It was the last put down I was ever going to hear from them. It was awful to see my own family working so hard to be counterproductive to what I was trying to accomplish in life. Just thinking about that exhausts the energy in me. My life was nothing but a big game to them and they played that way too long. By doing that, they were rewriting my script. They put their energy in all the wrong places. Over exerting their opinions onto me. I was validated by the psychologist who was my doctor, and the officer I spoke to. I know that I'm alive and well. I have arrived. I'm here.

Chapter 21

Just before I left Indiana in 1986, I was getting my belongings ready to be shipped out to Arizona before me. Sinead O'Connor had a real big hit written by Prince during that time. It was called "Nothing Compares 2U." I remember stopping by Dora's house to say goodbye just before I left for Arizona. She really didn't care. She was glad to see me going. In fact, both she and her husband started yelling at me. I forgot what for. I'm sure I really didn't pay attention. I still have a couple of pieces of my furniture that I bought with my first paycheck from the steel plant. Yes, they are quite collectible pieces now. My daughter recently took one of them. The oak roll top desk that was made in the Carolinas is one she took and that is circa 1970's. Perhaps before.

Ann had an important role to play in bringing me back to earth or helping to keep me grounded as I was ever going to be. When I was living back in Indiana, Ann and I hung out a lot together. She worked as a switchboard operator at the same hospital where I worked at one time. I eventually ended up working for the steel plant as a keypunch operator. The man who interviewed was the manager for that department. I think he read my application and felt sorry for me and gave me a break. Back then, some of the applications asked for our father's name, mother's maiden name, and grandmother's name. It was just weird.

Even where a person banked was a question. Ann and I would go to the mall, the lake, clubs, and concerts. I hung around with her to be safe and she cared about my wellbeing. She did more for me than my own family did. Disco was starting to become very popular then. *Saturday Night Live* was really popular. A lot of people watched that show. I remember the original cast members such as John Belushi, Dan Aykroyd, Gilda Radner, Lorraine New-man, Jane Curtin, and Chevy Chase to name a few.

. . . . .

Ann didn't care much for my sisters. She was an excellent judge of character. I really admired her. I think we were about 22 years old when Ann told me that my sisters were jealous of me. I dismissed that because I didn't want to believe that. They were the only family I had, back then I used to think, some are better than none. Albeit, I never trusted them, and didn't feel safe with them either. I envied her judgment of character because she was always right. I didn't have that trait within myself being dissociated.

Being dissociated, I didn't have much conversation with anyone. I was extremely shy. If I had a conversation at all, it centered on music and the artists. Even when I lived alone, I just listened to music. If it weren't for music, I wouldn't have had a conversation at all. I always lived alone and would do things by myself. A person I knew from the steel plant once said to me that I was the only person she knew who could enjoy my own company. I just learned to live that way. My family had little to no contact with me. They sure didn't want me around. The only contact was when they wanted something from me. If I wasn't with Ann, I'd be completely alone in my hometown. I admired how Ann could have a lengthy conversation with someone. A few words about music and that was it for me. I spent most of my days alone.

Ann and I went on a couple of vacations. We went to Las Vegas once. It was for three days and four nights. Another friend of Ann's was traveling with us. We stayed at the MGM Grand Hotel. We were in an elevator there when the door opened up behind us and led right into the room of B.J. Thomas. He and his band were getting ready to leave to go play in the lounge. He gave us an autographed picture. Another time we took a bus to California just for fun. We went from Indiana to California in two and a half days. We stayed with an older brother of mine and his wife while we were there. They lived in a small town outside of Sacramento. We were gone for two weeks. My brother's wife let us use her MG car to go to Reno. They also took us to Lake Tahoe to a dinner club where we saw Tom Jones. We all spend the night there. Ann and I shared a hotel room. We went to a casino and locked ourselves out of that room. Some guys we met at the Casino broke the lock for us to get in. The hotel manager was really mad and Ann and I had to pay for the broken lock.

We took a bus to San Francisco during our stay there. We went to Fisherman's Wharf and Chinatown. We started to run low on funds. We decided to stay the night in a cheap hotel. The hotel was on Poke Street and had torn white plastic curtains flying out of the windows. When we checked in at the lobby, I saw the old paint-chipped, gated, metal elevator stop.

I said, *"Ann, the elevator stopped—let's take it up to the room."*

She looked and said, "I'm not getting in there!"

I looked again and saw there was a man who had blood all over him and had some kind of club or stick in his hand. That was the dissociated me not giving danger any real thought.

We waited for the next ride to go up to our room. I'm surprised we didn't run out of there. There was a community bathroom and a shower. We took turns sleeping that night and left the next day to go back to my brother's house. We took an airplane back to Indiana. When we looked back at that, we both laughed a lot.

Ann and I were at a club one night. The year was 1974. We went to the bathroom and ended up walking out through their kitchen. We saw silverware just brought out of the dishwasher. It was just lying there and no one was around. I did eventually have silverware for my first apartment. Ann and I laughed our way out to her car.

Even though I was dissociated, Ann shared many laughs with me. She was a true friend. We really did have fun. I'd just do things she did. I'd go to places with her because I felt safe with her. Whenever we went places, she had the whole event organized. I would let her do all the talking. She really looked out for me.

The last couple of years in Indiana, Ann was really getting involved with a young man and I hardly saw her at all. I was beginning to think her bachelorette days were coming to an end. It had been two years since I heard from Zachery. The night before I left for Arizona, Ann and I met at a club that was close to Marie's house. Ann was quiet and looked really sad. I think she felt my pain for me, thinking I was going to have to start all over. We walked out and over to our cars. I told her that I'd keep in touch and we parted ways.

. . . . .

We reconnected many years after I left my hometown. I was busy in Arizona trying to keep my head above water. I called Ann to tell her about my freedom from dissociation. She had fallen very ill at that particular time. So, I never got to tell her. She told me she heard rumors about me. The rumors made by my two elder sisters back in my hometown. When I was correcting some of the rumors she stopped me by saying, *"I hate your sisters."* I think she really hated what they did to me. I could tell she saw the whole picture before I was done speaking. One of the rumors she heard was that I had a lot of psychological problems. It was Darla and Dora doing that. Ann was always defending me saying to others, *"There's nothing wrong with Graci—I know her."* There were many times she thought I wasn't paying attention. That goes all the way back to our school girl days. That's how much localized amnesia dissociative disorder is hidden. It's not visible to the human eye. The only psychological problem I had was the result of being born into my family.

Just before Ann died, we had one of our last conversations together over the phone. I knew her health was failing. We both laughed a lot and were telling each other things about each other we never said before. She told me that when we'd go to a club, she'd hurry and walk in the door in front of me. She said she wanted to be seen first. She thought that if I walked in first, no one would see her. I say that's simply not true. Ann was a really cute girl! She didn't have to do that. I told her how I envied her skills of judging people so accurately and how good she was at starting conversations. I thought that was much more important. We both laughed reminiscing over old times. After we hung up, I cried. I sent her one last letter but I didn't get a response.

Her son called me a couple of weeks later and said, *"My mother gave me a list of people she wanted me to call when she passed. Your name was on the top of the list. My mother has a photo album filled with just pictures of you and her."* He said, she would say, *"The lake was mine and Graci's stomping grounds."* Back in the 1970s, the lake was where all the hippies would hang out. I was with Ann right in the middle of that. Just moving around not knowing what I was doing.

I held back the tears. I wouldn't have made it in my hometown if it hadn't been for Ann. She really looked out for me and will always be in my heart.

· · · · ·

For some that had tougher blows than others in life, we have to learn to love and embrace the damaged child within. That will always be a part of me. Changing what I can and accepting what I cannot change was my determination. What I can change, I did. What I couldn't change, I learned to change my thoughts about it. I keep communications open with Melissa. My family here is functional. I'm only glad that I had Barry in my life to help with the child rearing of Melissa. He was a hands-on dad. I learned a lot of great parenting skills from this wonderful person and what it's like to unconditionally love.

He did a fine job with Melissa. They have always had a very close relationship. By the time she was two years old he taught her the basic colors. She did a fine job in school as well and was exceptional in math and music. She plays four instruments—piano, violin, sax, and guitar. Her major in college was science. She's our brag and yes, she is a scientist. She had our support there, too. She's a lot like Barry when it comes to chemistry and math. We both talk to her a lot. She enjoyed having me with her in her school during her elementary years. Her aunt on her dad's side has a wonderful relationship with her as well. Melissa is a lot like her aunt. She's cute when she sounds like her aunt sometimes, in a "so matter of fact" way. She took responsibilities on her own at a young age. Working after high school when she turned sixteen was a big milestone for her. She turned into a very responsible young lady. Her group of friends were all in the gifted classes. These were all very smart and fine children. I became friends with some of their parents and we carpooled when they went to junior high. That was really nice and I enjoyed being a mom then. By high school they didn't want us around anymore. Melissa went off to college in her pursuit of higher education and majored in science, chemistry, and biology. Both Barry and I couldn't be prouder of her. I thank my lucky stars for Barry. What patience he has. I learned quite a bit from this beautiful man both inside and out. He has been a good influence in my life. I know why my sisters were after him. Not only them but others too.

Chapter 22

It's easy to describe now, but in the first session with the doctor, I didn't know how or where to start. I just started talking about how I left and came back after a really long time. I didn't know how to start that. He wasn't satisfied with my statement that I left and came back after a long time. He wanted to know more. Thank goodness he led that conversation. I was telling him about my social work class and the flash I had. When I told him about Dora traumatizing me is when he asked, with a sadness in his voice, *"What did they want you to do?"* It was as if he knew what I went through over many years. I started out in life as a precocious four year old. They have no idea the magnitude of damage they did to me that night. That little four year old went away and didn't come back until she was an older adult as a social worker and a mandated reporter.

While talking to the doctor in sessions, I didn't make the connection with music, my writing where ma played the piano and pa would sing, and feeling. He made the comment that music evokes a lot of feelings. I agree. I didn't connect that. Not right then I didn't. He made that connection for me. A lot of the connecting that he did hit me while I was writing this. He was connecting everything for me. I just thought I was lucky to have remembered it. I was telling him about the prayer I did in 1986 where I asked for feelings. That's when he told me that emotions are a very big part of dissociation. I didn't think that audio and visual senses had an important role in helping me to remember the biggest scene of that traumatic night so long ago. The rest of the scenes that came to me were smaller ones surrounding the big scene. They might have been small but were the pieces that I had to join together in order for me to solve this puzzle of my dissociation. All those years that horrible night was kept a secret. That secret transcended over time and is still going on today. A secret that tore my family apart and rendered us extremely dysfunctional. We are a broken family.

· · · · ·

Sitting at work, taking calls from the help line call center, I was asked to go into a meeting. My higher-ups were trying to find what crime I was committing. Well, I wasn't doing anything wrong. My higher-ups were also asking me questions about the job, I answered them and then some. I think Darla and Robert were saying that I didn't know anything and not to trust me with any work. I loved my job and my performance was enough to show it. Who the hell did they think they were? They were going up against a person with a master's degree. I think everyone in that particular department has a degree and most are at the master level. I know the manager wasn't pleased with what Robert was doing and that showed. Darla and Robert were really closing in on me. That had such an emotional impact on me. That started to carry over into my work. Robert just thought he was above everyone. Darla too. She morphed into a super being beyond reproach. So she thought. So did he. Their actions were pitiful. I knew I had to talk to someone and saw the doctor after all of this. It was said to me, "He who laughs last..." I didn't take that literally either. I took that as an unpleasant and quite angered remark over what they were doing to me. There is nothing funny about what they were doing to me. And that remark was said to me more than once. It was after all of this that the Doctor and Officer intervened. They were both divine intervention. It was then that Dora, Darla and Robert's game was over. I for sure lost that battle. I know it's always better to win the war.

It was a drill. Darla found out where I worked and what agency. She then told her husband who would begin his networking thing. My life was a big game to them. With a serious game like that, there's always a chance of someone losing. Something had to be done to put an end to all of the nonsense, meanness, and madness. They were feeding their egos off of me. Darla was using her best connections, too. Dora was in there with Darla. I would often wonder, *"Who would believe me?"* Not only did I want to stop her from hurting my life, but there were others out there that were at potential risk. That included our daughter.

Shortly after that last work related incident, I went to see the doctor. Knowing that I had once left as a four years old, I wasn't willing to go through even a bit of it again. I knew I didn't return for a long time and now I wasn't a lone wolf, but had a family. I knew I had to return to bring my life together and protect it from coming apart again, the way it did when I was four years old. I didn't know how I was to do that, but I realized that I had to speak to somebody of the right caliber about it. Someone who would think outside the box. Someone smart and intuitive. Someone who would give me a voice because what I had to say mattered.

The sessions with the doctor gave me the knowledge and confidence I needed to follow through with that phone call, and so I did. That marked the beginning of my freedom. I called my hometown police and just hoped I got the right person. That call wasn't easy for me either. I kept talking. I didn't stop. I told everything I remembered from that night. I didn't leave any stone unturned. There was too much of a chance that something could go bad. I didn't want to leave anyone at risk.

After we hung up, I felt a sense of calmness come over me as though I just took my power back from my evil sisters. I didn't hear anything anymore from any of the sisters that were doing mean things to me. Darla and the others were silenced. Neither she, nor evil Dora, are in any position of harming me anymore. My daughter is also safe from them. The last thing I know of Darla and her husband is that they now live somewhere in the Midwest.

The Cadillac SUV wasn't the only thing Rosey told me about. She later called and revealed, *"Darla's getting her master's degree in math. She's starting out with a couple of classes."*

I responded in an exhausted voice, *"She needs to stop competing with me. She just needs to go live her life."* I would have been right to say, *Tell her to take Robert with her. They might get something out of that.* But I didn't. I'll just keep that to myself.

Sometimes I think she always thought she had to do better than me because she was older. That stems from childhood days. She was like that back then. Her case with the boys was no different. She only wanted the ones I had. She'd come up behind me and try to pass me up. Now I know how she was doing that. She'd knock me down verbally in front of others exposing my every weakness, whatever it was. She'd do this thinking I'd never know because I wasn't paying attention. Then she'd come in behind me like a hero. That phase went on throughout my life until I remembered and stopped them. I think I stopped them. Given the chance, they'll probably still try to harm me. I'm not worried though. Not like I was before. At times, I used to wonder how she was able to pull off being married to who she was married to for so many years. Now I know. I can't help but to think that he is just like her. Maybe they're two of a kind.

Now maybe she'll get some help. I don't think she will though. A later phone call from Rosey revealed, in a calm manner, *"Darla says she's all right and doesn't think about that anymore. She doesn't care about what happened 100 years ago."* She lacks insight there and I don't think she has the capacity to look at her life introspectively. It's still going on today. She's a fractured child trapped in an adult body. They wanted to do what I did. They didn't want to do the work I did to get to where I'm at. I did what they didn't want to do. That goes for all of those involved in taking me down. They all thought they were entitled to take what I had. They were trying to take what I worked hard for. To accomplish higher education takes a lot of physical and mental stamina. I place a very high value on higher education and put a lot of hard work into that. On a scale of one to ten, with ten being the highest, education is right up there. Second only to God and my family. Think of how differently this would have turned out if Darla put her energy into getting help for herself many years ago. She would have been much better off today. We all would. I did what I had to do. That had to stop and for me it did.

· · · · ·

Now I don't even hear from Rosey anymore. It's been really quiet. I don't hear from anyone at all. It's kind of nice not having them following me around.

They don't try to make my life miserable either. They are all consumed by their own problems—the problems they rightfully own.

I am a retired social worker and live in the Southwest with my family. I will advocate against those who practice any sorts of injustice. I will not limit myself to fighting against child abuse and domestic violence but shall stand against any kind of injustice to my full capacity. Life is so nice, but only if others do not make us suffer. In my case, the people who wanted me to continue paying for what happened to them, didn't play their cards right. I, in the process, learned that only the truth can and will set you free. I had to have patience because the truth does take time to emerge. I sometimes wish that it hadn't taken so long. I wasted a lot of my life trying to grow into myself. I won't question that though because things happen for a reason. I'm glad it at least happened in this lifetime of mine. I will never stop learning. I truly love learning!

The nature of this content is never an easy topic to talk about. It wasn't easy for me either. However, it really does need to be brought to light. Keeping secrets of child abuse will only hold a person back in attaining their full potential. Bringing secrets of child abuse to the forefront to be dealt with properly, will aid in prevention and heighten awareness. In our family that needed to be talked about and dealt with appropriately. Bringing dissociation to the table will hopefully help others to recognize this debilitating illness and enlighten others on how to remedy this phenomenon so a person doesn't loose themselves in the world. It's never a good idea to operate from only one side of the story either. For one thing, it's way too overbalanced. During one of my later sessions with the doctor, after he answered my life long question as to who I am, I thought and said, *"I will learn to love and embrace the damaged child within."* He responded, *"Well spoken!"* That I have done and the twist of fate that was brought on by the intervention was nothing short of poetic justice.